The Ghosts of Williamsburg

Volume II

by L. B. Taylor, Jr.

Fourth Printing
2010

Photographs by the Author
Illustrations by
Brenda Goens

ISBN 1-928966-00-4

CONTENTS

AUTHOR'S NOTE IV

INTRODUCTION VI

WILLIAMSBURG

1. RETURN TO PEYTON RANDOLPH HOUSE 1

2. THE HAUNTING HOSTESS OF KING'S ARMS TAVERN . . . 6

3. BLACKBEARD AND HIS GHOSTLY PIRATES. 11

4. PHANTOM SOUNDS AT THE PUBLIC GAOL. 15

5. THE LEGEND OF LADY ANN SKIPWITH - PART II 19

6. THE MYSTERY LADY OF THE GHOST TOUR. 24

7. THE MISSING VAULT AT BRUTON
   PARISH CHURCH 27

8. THE MYSTIQUE SURROUNDING MATTHEW
   WHALEY'S DEATH 33

9. THE APPARITIONAL RETURN OF
   CUTHBERT OGLE 36

10. REMINISCENCES AT THE RALEIGH TAVERN 39

11. A SAMPLING OF SPECTRAL VIGNETTES. 42
    — The 'See-Through' Man at Tarpley's Store 42
    — Red Eyes Shining in the Dark 42
    — Night Noises in the Travis House 44
    — Miss Gibbie Galt's Secret Room 44
    — A Loving Spirit at the Palace. 45
    — Stripped Beds at the Lightfoot House 47
    — A Curious Crowd at the Capitol 48
    — A Pair of Ghostly Babysitters 49
    — What Secrets Lurk at the Williamsburg Inn? 50

— The 'Barrel Man' of the Bluebell Tavern 51
— The House Where Time Stood Still 52

12. THE STAGE STRUCK SPECTER AT
    WILLIAM AND MARY 54

13. FURTHER REVELATIONS AT CARTER'S GROVE 58

14. THE FEARFUL FORCE AT CROAKER 63

JAMESTOWN

15. THE FIRST SPIRITS IN VIRGINIA? 67

16. CAUGHT IN A COLONIAL TIME WARP 73

17. IS JAMESTOWN ISLAND FOREVER CURSED? 76

18. THE CHARISMATIC CAVALIER AND THE
    VENGEFUL GOVERNOR 81

19. A HOST OF HAUNTING HUMOR 86
    — Five Figures Rising in the Mist 86
    — Aunt Pratt Strikes Again 87
    — Escape Attempt from an Open Grave 89
    — Never Make Fun of a Ghost 90
    — The Curious Funeral of Billy Gilliam 91
    — Painting an Apparition Black 92
    — Say that Again 92
    — It Must Be Hell 92

YORKTOWN

20. MORE HISTORIC HAUNTINGS AT THE
    MOORE HOUSE 93

21. ACTIVE SPIRITS AT THE COLE-DIGGES HOUSE 96
    — The Ghost Coach of Black Swamp . . . .

22. WHO HAUNTS CORNWALLIS' GRAVE? 101

23. AN EXORCISM (OR TWO) AT THE NELSON HOUSE . . . 106

24. THE JEALOUS BARKEEP OF YORKTOWN 109

'PLANTATION ROW'

25. THE FURTHER ETHEREAL RETURNS OF
MISS EVELYN BYRD 116

26. THE DAUNTING DREAMS OF WILLIAM BYRD, II 124

27. BIZARRE HAPPENINGS AT BERKELEY. 127

28. THE 'LEGEND' OF RIPPON'S HOLLOW 134

29. THE 'GRAY LADY' OF SHERWOOD FOREST - PART II . . 139

30. THE 'PEOPLE OF THE HOUSE' AT COLESVILLE. 143

31. THE GHOSTLY REENACTMENT OF
JEB STUART'S RIDE 147

32. THE CONFEDERATE SOLDIER WHO DIED TWICE! 153

33. SKULL & CROSSBONES 160
— Odds and Ends of the Curious and Unexplained 160

ACROSS THE JAMES RIVER

34. MORE BAFFLING REVELATIONS AT
BACON'S CASTLE 167

35. SOMETHING THAT 'SWOOSHED' AT CHIPPOKES 170

36. UNACCOUNTABLE EVENTS AT UPPER BRANDON 172

37. A TRAGIC TOAST AT BRANDON 178

ABOUT THE AUTHOR 183

Author's Note:

In 1982 my editor at Simon & Schuster in New York asked me to write a book on "Haunted Houses." In doing the research, two things happened. One, I became fascinated with the general subject of psychic phenomena, and specifically with ghosts. And, two, I discovered a wealth of absorbing material on the subjects here in the Commonwealth of Virginia — far more than I could include in one brief book covering the whole country.

So I decided to write and publish a book on my own about Williamsburg ghosts. My editor said I was crazy, that regional books don't do well. I did it anyway. The original "Ghosts of Williamsburg" was printed in 1983. It has been successful beyond expectations. It has sold more than 100,000 copies.

In the next 10 years, between 1983 and 1992, I published four more regional books on area haunts: "The Ghosts of Richmond;" "The Ghosts of Tidewater;" "The Ghosts of Fredericksburg;" and "The Ghosts of Charlottesville and Lynchburg." All have gone into multiple printings.

In 1993 the entire state was covered in "The Ghosts of Virginia." When that came out I thought I was through with the topic. I had used all the material in my files. Then a strange thing happened. People began calling and writing letters to me telling of their ethereal experiences. Whenever I gave a talk (about 25 or 30 a year), men, women and children would come up afterwards to share a paranormal encounter they had, or to tell of a "new" haunted house.

Thus came "The Ghosts of Virginia," volumes II, III, IV, and, soon, V, plus "Civil War Ghosts of Virginia." It all added up to close to one million words. This heartfelt interest in the area's ghost lore and legend continues to amaze me. Virginians do want to know of their storied past, which is in danger of being trampled into oblivion by the high-tech, electronic, televised, computerized age we live in. And these rich traditions, some dating to the earliest settlers, are a colorful and, at times, an educational part of our heritage. They are priceless heirlooms of commonwealth history that need to be preserved.

The fascination of the combination of local history with the supernatural may best be calculated in the enormous popularity of ghost tours that now are conducted in all parts of Virginia. Here in Williamsburg, for example, the original tour, started more than a decade ago and based on my book, draws close to 100,000 people a year.

For the past several years, I have been frequently asked when am I going to update "The Ghosts of Williamsburg." Why should I? After all, that book has done well, so "why fix it if it ain't broken?" True, over the years, considerable fresh material surfaced. More ghosts were found through personal interviews, in old family histories and diaries, in ancient magazine articles and long out of print tomes, and through other sources.

Finally, it dawned on me. Why not leave the first book alone, and do a separate volume II? This is the result. A few of the original chapters, such as the Peyton Randolph House, the Wythe House and Sherwood Forest have been updated and expanded with new information. Other chapters cover houses, plantation homes and sites not found in volume I. Some of these chapters have appeared in the "Ghosts of Virginia" series, but here are edited, collected and packaged in one book. In addition to Williamsburg, volume II includes ghostly "appearances" at Jamestown, Yorktown, "Plantation Row," in Charles City County, between Williamsburg and Richmond, and additional houses just across the James River. Many of the homes are among the most historic in Virginia, and most are open to the public.

As with all the books in this series, (there are now 11), it has been a true labor of love to research and write them. I have a passion for Virginia history, and this continuing project has afforded me the opportunity to visit scores of interesting houses, meet many fascinating people, and learn more about our glorious past. It has been a most joyful and enriching venture.

Introduction

Are there such things as ghosts? Is there a veiled nether world somewhere between earth and the hereafter. Do some departed souls get trapped in between and occasionally make themselves known to those of us still living?

Does anyone, including psychic experts, really know? After all, we have been arguing about the existence of ghosts for the past 5,000 years or so, and a definitive solution is yet to be found. Some believe, some don't believe, and many just aren't sure.

If there are ghosts, who and what are they? Experts say they are the spirits of those who have died, usually tragically and/or traumatically, but are unaware of their deaths. But definitions can run the gamut. A professor at the University of Iowa once said ghosts are people who have died and "missed the bus." Perhaps one of the best answers was offered by Henry Price of Oxford University. He said if ghosts exist, they do so in a "dimension or dimensions unknown to us."

Why are there so many ghosts in Williamsburg, Jamestown, Yorktown, and the surrounding area? Perhaps because so much tragedy has occurred here — from the Indian massacres of the early 1600s to the battles of the Revolutionary and Civil Wars. And there are so many old houses here, habitats ghosts seem to find comfortable.

The Reverend Dr. W. A. R. Goodwin is the man most responsible for the modern restoration of Colonial Williamsburg. In the late 1920s he convinced philanthropist John D. Rockefeller, Jr., to spend millions of dollars to preserve a most important segment of American history—to rebuild and restore the town that served as the colonial capital of Virginia from 1699 to 1780. It was a massive undertaking, but today, each year, more than a million tourists come to Colonial Williamsburg to see what life was like here in the 18th century.

Dr. Goodwin once wrote Rockefeller a letter. In it, he said: "In Williamsburg we always have the ghosts which abide, even when the distinguished men of the present come, stay for a day, and depart. I have always felt sorry for the people who live in Williamsburg who are incapable of holding companionship with the ghosts."

Of course, Dr. Goodwin's comment is open to wide interpretation. Some, however, believe he was speaking more than just figuratively.

Whatever, here then is a second volume on "The Ghosts of Williamsburg," combining colorful anecdotes and vignettes of history with haunting legend and lore.

Enjoy!

This book is for
Brenda Goens

Return to Peyton Randolph House

(Author's note: One of the first chapters I wrote on Williamsburg ghosts concerned a phantom-like vision which several witnesses said appeared at the foot of their bed in an oak-paneled upstairs bedroom at historic Peyton Randolph House in Colonial Williamsburg. The wraith, in the wispy apparitional form of a woman, apparently materialized on infrequent occasions to certain startled guests who believed she, or "it," was there to warn them of some impending tragedy. I called the chapter, "The Nagging Shrew of Peyton Randolph House."

It included the background history of the building, which dates to about 1715, and gave some information on Peyton Randolph, who was, among other things, president of the first Continental Congress, and one of the principal leaders of the American cause for freedom. Interestingly, when Randolph died in 1775 of an apoplectic stroke, Thomas Jefferson bought his library. Randolph's and Jefferson's collection later became the nucleus of the Library of Congress.

While doing the original research on the house I virtually ran into a stone wall. Historical interpreters who gave tours here flatly wouldn't discuss the subject of ghosts. Eventually, however, a few Colonial Williamsburg employees did talk about the hauntings "off the record." I then wrote: "Of those who know the house well, none doubt that there is something inexplicably strange about it. Too many people have experienced similar eerie phenomena within its walls."

Peyton Randolph House

I also said that the house, over the generations, "had slowly gained notoriety as a residence of sadness and tragedy. Many people met strange and untimely deaths there during the 19th and 20th centuries." This, in fact, was true. Several children had died in the house, some in bizarre accidents, and there was evidence there had been some suicides there.

Soon after the book came out, in 1983, the Virginia Gazette reprinted the Peyton Randolph chapter on page one. It was then that I got a phone call one evening from an elderly lady, who shall remain nameless, who had grown up and <u>still lived</u> in the house! For the next hour or so, she gave me the worst tongue lashing I have ever received. She said in no uncertain terms, that I was utterly mistaken; that she had lived there since childhood and it definitely was not a sad house! She had always been happy there.

Today, however, things are a little different. The enormous popularity of the nightly Williamsburg ghost tour, on which the Peyton Randolph House is a key stop, has loosened the reluctance of some to talk about the haunting encounters they have experienced.

For instance, in May 1995, I got a letter from a lady named Aria Smith who lives in Berkeley, California. She took a Colonial

Williamsburg tour called "Legends of the Past," with, as she said, "the hopes that the guide might discuss some of the stories of ghosts that haunt the Wythe House or the Peyton Randolph House, but not a word was mentioned about them."

Determined, Ms. Smith took the tour guide aside and asked her directly about the ghosts. "She confirmed that the employees believe Peyton Randolph to be haunted, saying that the house had been 'difficult' recently."

Only two days earlier, another employee had shared with the guide a hair-raising personal experience, which occurred at Christmas-time in 1994. This employee was responsible for the lighted decorations there. Early one morning, during the holiday season, she entered the house as usual, to attend to the lights. She was singing a Christmas carol to herself. As she came into the house, she saw a black woman, in colonial dress, seated at the foot of the stairs, swaying from side to side in time with the carol. The worker, not wanting to disturb her, began to step around her, but as she looked back, the swaying woman was gone!

There's more. I attended a Civil War reenactment at Jamestown a few years ago and had a long conversation with a young man named Kent Brinkley, who is a landscape architect at Colonial Williamsburg. Kent knew the lady who had lived at the Peyton Randolph House over the past half century or so and he said she had related some curious incidents which had happened to *her!*)

Once, when she was 13-years-old, she was sleeping alone in one of the bedrooms (it wasn't specified if this was the oak-paneled room.) She awoke to see the image of a "teenage girl peeking at her." The girl was wearing a white nightgown, and the resident thought at first her sister was playing a trick on her and she called out, but got no response. Unnerved, she got out of her bed and went to her parents' room. They were asleep. She then went to her sister's room, crawled in bed with her, and declared she wasn't about to go back into her own room that night!

On another occasion the woman was alone in the house washing dishes. Her mother and sister had gone to a coffee shop. She heard footsteps upstairs and thought maybe her mother and sister had forgotten something and returned. So she went upstairs to check. There was no one there! She looked out the window, and the family car was gone. She went back to the kitchen, but heard the same sounds three or four different times. This was too much for her. She called the coffee shop and told her mother to immediately come and get her. She didn't want to stay in the house alone.

In yet another incident, a Colonial Williamsburg maintenance man was in the basement one day when the house was closed to the public. He was there to work on the furnace. The woman who lived there heard a knock on her back door. She opened it and there was the maintenance man, she said, "as white as a sheet." He told her he had been in the cellar working when he heard someone mumbling. He looked around, but saw nothing. He said the mumbling grew progressively louder.

Finally, he turned around again and froze. He said he saw a black man, dressed in colonial costume, shaking his finger at him. He spoke to the figure, saying, "it's okay, I work for Colonial Williamsburg." He said the strange figure then disappeared.

The woman told him he could come back another day to finish his work. He looked at her blankly, then stammered, "Lady, there ain't going to be a next time!" He left the house and never returned.

And, finally, there is an account that could be classified as a crisis apparition which occurred in Peyton Randolph House some time ago. A custodial worker was in the house alone early one morning, cleaning. The house had not yet been opened to the public for the day. The woman was startled at seeing a tour hostess in her colonial costume suddenly appear standing at the top of the stairs. The worker wondered what the woman was doing there so early. She hadn't seen her come in and she hadn't heard the door opening or closing.

Besides, this particular hostess had retired. Why was she here? Just as quickly, the vision of the lady evaporated. A little later, other employees entered the house. One of them told her that a former hostess had just died. The custodial worker stared at her in fright. It was the same woman she had seen at the top of the stairs that morning! The worker then tore out of the house as fast as she could.

The question is, who are these ghosts and why have they returned to this particular house? Did they suffer a tragic death? Why does the nagging shrew appear at bedside as if to warn? There seems to be no rational clue as to the identity of what may be several spirits.

One might suspect to see the apparitions of Peyton Randolph

himself, and his brother John. As the seeds of the American Revolution were sprouting in the early and mid 1770s, Peyton became a staunch exponent of the cause of liberty, while John remained a bitter and resolute loyalist and supporter of the King of England. It must have torn the brothers apart.

When Peyton died in 1775, he was buried inside a chapel at the College of William and Mary. John, disgruntled and disheartened with what he considered the tyrannical events unfolding in the colonies, fled to England that same year. When he died, nine years later, his remains were brought back to Virginia and buried beside his brother's. Wouldn't that somehow justify their spectral reappearance at the house to continue the heated debate they left unsettled in life?

So many questions, so few answers.

CHAPTER 2

The Haunting Hostess at the King's Arms Tavern

(Author's Note: I got a call one night in April 1997 from a tour and convention booking agency. They asked if I would conduct a ghost tour of Colonial Williamsburg. There is a nightly ghost tour, but this was to be a one-time special event. I thought it might be fun so I agreed. We walked up and down historic Duke of Gloucester Street and talked about the alleged haunts on the campus of the College of William and Mary, at the Peyton Randolph House, the George Wythe House, the Ludwell-Paradise House, and so forth. We wound up at the King's Arms Tavern, one of several such dining establishments in the colonial area.

While bidding my adieus in the entrance area at the tavern, a young man saw me holding a copy of my book, "The Ghosts of Williamsburg," and, after one of the tour executives introduced us, he announced that "we have a ghost here at the King's Arms!" He then proceeded to tell me about it.)

To get a literal flavor of the foods of Colonial Williamsburg — typical of some of the fare served more than 200 years ago to such notables as George Washington and General Thomas Nelson of Yorktown, one might opt to dine at the King's Arms Tavern. It is considered one of the most "genteel" of the 18th century restaurants in Williamsburg. Featured on the menu are such old Virginia staples as peanut soup, country ham, Southern-style fried chicken, game pie and Sally

Lunn bread. There is also an oyster-stuffed filet mignon, Cavalier's lamb, and apple cheddar muffins. Desserts include pecan pie, meringue shell and "Grand Trifle" — a sherry-soaked sponge cake with vanilla custard and dark cherries. It has been a British favorite since the 17th century.

On February 6, 1772, an enterprising young woman named Jane Vobe ran the following advertisement in the Williamsburg Gazette: "I have just opened TAVERN opposite to the Raleigh (Tavern) at the sign of the KING'S ARMS. . . and shall be much obliged to the Gentlemen who favour me with their company." She apparently was successful from the start. During the Revolutionary War Mrs. Vobe supplied food and drink to American troops, and it is said that Baron von Steuben ran up a bill of nearly 300 Spanish dollars for lodging, meals and beverages. It is not specified whether or not he paid such a bill. For years, the tavern served as a popular local gathering place where customers met to discuss business, politics, news and gossip. Artifacts found on the site and sketches of the building, drawn on late 18th century insurance policies, assisted in the authentic reconstruction of the King's Arms. Today, there are 11 separate dining rooms with seating for up to 250 people.

Whether or not one encounters a haunting experience there, however, is chancy. The ghost appears only infrequently, and mostly to Colonial Williamsburg employees and not to guest diners. One might suspect the female phantom who has been reported there to be Jane Vobe herself. But this ghost apparently is one of much more recent vintage. Some believe it, in fact, may be the return of a former manager of the tavern — a woman named Irma.

"She lived here years ago," says former assistant manager Jeffrey Pilley. "In those days they didn't serve in the upstairs rooms and these were used as her apartment. We had a lead hostess here named Betty. She was here for 40 years. Well, the story, as I got it, was that Betty would come in on Saturday mornings, go up to Irma's apartment, and the two of them would read the newspapers together.

"One Saturday morning Betty came in, but she said she couldn't go upstairs to the apartment that day. She didn't know specifically why, but she steadfastly refused. So an assistant manager went upstairs. He got no answer to repeated knocks on the door. Then he stooped down to look through the keyhole. Irma was lying on the floor. She had died."

Jeffrey says that since then there have been a number of inex-

King's Arms Tavern

plicable things that have occurred at the tavern. Trays fall off stands when no one is around. Candles are extinguished by unseen hands or breath even though they are protected by glass globes. Menus sometimes topple out of wall stands.

Jeffrey has had his own encounters. "I've never seen her," he says, "but there are some things that happen." Once when he was closing up and standing outside with a night host, he looked up and saw that a window upstairs was wide open. "I went up about half past eleven to close it," Jeffrey says, "but when I got there it was not only closed but locked as well. I thought the host had done it, but he said he hadn't. There was no one else in the place."

At other times, when alone in the King's Arms, Jeffrey has felt a peculiar chill. "I have felt the hair on the back of my neck stand up. One night in particular, I had this chill in every room I went in, upstairs and down, as I was closing up. When I got to the front door I turned around and said, 'Irma, leave me alone!' Just as I did the chill was suddenly gone and I felt a warm feeling wash over me. It was kind of eerie."

Others have told Jeffrey they have seen Irma, or at least the apparition of a woman. One hostess said she was upstairs in the women's rest room washing her hands. She heard the door open and when she looked in the mirror there was a lady standing behind her. She reached for a towel and turned around. There was no one there and the door had not been reopened.

On another occasion a hostess and a pantry worker both saw the appearance of a woman dressed in colonial costume. They said she had long flowing gray hair. At first they thought she was a balladeer, there to entertain the guests. But then, to their astonishment, the woman walked through a door. Jeffrey asked them what they meant. They told him the woman didn't open the door and pass through — she walked through the closed door! Still another hostess told of feeling a gentle shove in her back when she was at the top of the stairs one night. She skidded down the stairs but was unhurt.

Then one night a year or so ago, Jeffrey was standing on the porch at about nine o'clock when a woman, walking up the street, stopped in front of him and told him he had "interesting energy." She said she was a psychic from California. She asked him if she might go in the tavern to look around. There still were about 150 diners inside.

"She told me that 'George is here'," Jeffrey recalls. "Then she said no, he's not here, but he used to run this place. Jeffrey had not known any previous manager named George. "We went upstairs and as we started to walk into what is called the 'Gallery Room,' she stopped. It was like she had walked into a wall. She said, 'she's right here.' I said, 'who's here?' And she said it was a woman. She said she didn't see the woman, but she saw an aura around her. I didn't see it. Then the psychic told me that the woman was very happy and that she liked me. She said that I was good for the tavern. The psychic said the woman's name either started with an 'M,' or had an 'M' in it. At that time I hadn't known about Irma. The next day I asked Betty, the long-time hostess, had we had a previous manager who had an 'M' in her name and Betty then told me about Irma."

Jeffrey continues: "I later did some research, and found out that there had been three past assistant managers named George. Another thing the psychic had told me was that Irma would be there to help me if I ever needed help in the tavern. Some months later we had a group of 34 in one party and they all wanted to be seated in one room. We had a room upstairs that would hold 24, so I told them we could put 24 there and 10 in an adjoining room, but they refused. They insisted on all being together. Somehow, and I can't explain how to this day, I got all 34 in that one room, and they had a great time. We had never done that before and all the other workers thought I was crazy to try it. There wasn't room for 34, but I got them in and they were fine. Then I thought about what the psychic had told me — that Irma would help me. Maybe she did that night. I have to say Irma, or whoever she is, has been good to me. I say good night to her every night when I leave."

* * * * *

There is an interesting footnote to the ghost at the King's Arms Tavern. It was related to the author by the Reverend Dick Carter, a Virginia historical scholar who once worked at Colonial Williamsburg and now lives in Wakefield. He said that in the 1700s, when the colonial capital was located in Williamsburg, there used to be a lady who sold muffins at a spot between the King's Arms and Shields Tavern on Duke of Gloucester Street. She sold them to the gentlemen legislators as they made their way to the capitol building.

"You know," Dick says, "every time I walk by that spot, I swear I can smell the sweet scent of fresh muffins!"

Blackbeard and His Ghostly Pirates

hat does the notorious pirate Blackbeard have to do with Williamsburg? Actually, quite a bit.

— It was Governor Alexander Spotswood in Williamsburg in 1718 who dispatched a fleet of British war ships which led to a fierce battle causing the death of Blackbeard and several of his crew.

— A prevailing legend holds that Blackbeard's massive skull was later made into a drinking vessel used by thirsty imbibers at the Raleigh Tavern in Williamsburg.

— One of the more noted trials in Williamsburg's history found several members of Blackbeard's crew guilty of heinous crimes. They were hanged on the town's outskirts.

— There are witnesses who have reported hearing ghostly sounds of the executed pirates years, decades and even centuries after they were publicly executed.

Blackbeard, whose real name was either Edward Teach, Thatch, or Thach, reigned terror along the Virginia and North Carolina coast lines for years in the early 1700s. Of all the cutthroat pirates who sailed during these turbulent times, Blackbeard was considered the cruelest and most evil of all. He killed indiscriminately, and was feared not only by others sailing the coastal waters, but even by his own officers and crewmen.

He was a powerful and charismatic leader, and his abilities at swinging a cutlass were unmatched. It was said that he could slice a man in half with a single blow. And he loved to fight.

For a period of time, he literally ruled the coastlines, and, say many historians, gathered a vast treasure in stolen loot from all vessels that dared venture in his path. He was allegedly abetted by the governor of North Carolina, with whom he reportedly shared his bounty. Frustrated to the point of desperation, Governor Spotswood, in Williamsburg, commissioned several royal British ships to sail to Blackbeard's known hideout off Ocracoke Island in North Carolina.

Two of these sloops were commanded by Lieutenant Robert Maynard, and on the fateful day of November 22, 1718, a great battle ensued. Blackbeard and his men boarded Maynard's sloop. Single shot pistols fired and cutlasses clashed in ferocious hand-to-hand combat. Blackbeard himself was shot repeatedly and slashed by swords, yet fought on with a vicious vengeance. Donald Shomette, author of "Pirates on the Chesapeake," said, "Time after time he (Blackbeard) was struck, spewing blood and roaring imprecations as he stood his ground and fought with a great fury. One mighty arm swung his cutlass like a deadly windmill, while the other fired shot after shot from the brace of pistols in his bandolier. The sea about the sloop became literally tinctured with blood." Finally, after receiving five pistol shots and more than 20 other wounds, he fell dead on the deck of Maynard's sloop. The other pirates still standing soon surrendered.

Maynard then had Blackbeard's head severed and suspended it from the bowsprit of the sloop. According to a colorful legend, it was said that when the pirate leader's body was tossed overboard into the cold water, it defiantly swam around the ship several times before it sank.

When Maynard returned triumphantly to Virginia, the gruesome head was mounted on a high pole at the mouth of the Hampton River for many years as a warning to seafarers. The site is still known as "Blackbeard's Point."

The skull was later taken down and fashioned into the base of a large punch bowl, which, according to several authors, "was long used as a drinking vessel at the Raleigh Tavern in Williamsburg." Curiously, there are no reports of the headless ghost of Blackbeard returning. Some say perhaps he was pleased at what happened because Blackbeard himself loved nothing better than enjoying a well-filled punch bowl!

Lieutenant Maynard returned with 15 or 16 of the remaining pirates, (the number varies) to stand trial in the courts at

Blackbeard and his pirates

Williamsburg. There were no jurors, as this was not required under admiralty law. Since Governor Spotswood appointed the commissioners, the results were expected. All but one of the prisoners were convicted and sentenced to be hanged.

Samuel Odell was the only man acquitted. He had been aboard Blackbeard's ship only one day and had not participated in any villainous acts at sea. He had been caught by accident in the fighting and had sustained some 70 wounds. The court felt that was punishment enough.

Later, Israel Hands, a chief aide to Blackbeard, was pardoned. He died a beggar on the streets of London, and was later immortalized in Robert Louis Stevenson's classic, "Treasure Island."

In the spring of 1719, 13 (or 14) of the remaining pirates were ceremoniously taken by ox-drawn carts from the public gaol, down the streets of Williamsburg, riding atop their own coffins. They were transported to a site just off what is now known as Capitol Landing Road, but then was called Gallows Road. A large throng of townspeople gathered to witness the bizarre spectacle. Some brought picnic baskets.

And there, Blackbeard's crew members were swung into eternity.

But did they all depart? Over the centuries there have been persistent reports by citizens living in that area of hearing strange sounds on quiet, still nights . . . sounds of cart wheels creaking over the rutted roads . . . of the murmurings of a large crowd of people . . . and of the mournful moaning of condemned men ⸙

CHAPTER 4

Phantom Sounds at the Public Gaol

uring the trial of Blackbeard's pirates, the prisoners were held in Williamsburg's Public Gaol (pronounced jail). Of all the ancient buildings in the Colonial Capital (and this one dates to 1704), one might well suspect this would be the most haunted. It was the scene of the most horrible cruelties and suffering. Conditions, even by 18th century standards, were atrocious and inhumane.

Here, runaway slaves, murderers, cutthroats, pirates, marauding Indians, political and debtor prisoners, and even the criminally insane alike were shackled in heavy leg irons and handcuffs to await their fate, being decided in the nearby courts. It was thought by many that hanging was almost an "escape" from the harsh life one led in the overcrowded, rodent-infested building. In the frigid winters, prisoners shivered beneath thin, worm-eaten blankets. When food was served, it generally consisted of "damaged salt beef and Indian meal." Consequently, more inmates died from starvation and disease than ever reached the gallows.

Author Hildegarde Hawthorne, in her 1941 book, "Williamsburg Old and New," seemed depressed even when she visited the gaol. "The cells look terrifying today," she wrote. "So small, utterly unheated, no glass to the tiny, heavily barred windows, great iron rings riveted to the floor to which leg irons are attached, a heap of straw in one corner to sleep on . . . Scuttle-like openings in the walls, which are enormously thick, were used to shove food through to the prisoners. . ."

Hawthorne added that during the Revolutionary War things got particularly bad . . . "men being packed into the cells, the schedules of the Court upset, illness spreading fast with the increasing filth. Deserters, prisoners of war, Tories, spies, traitors, all met here."

One of the more infamous inmates here, in 1779, was Henry Hamilton, former governor-general of Detroit. He was called the "scalp taker," and the "hair buyer," because he was believed to have paid his Indian allies for American scalps.

The original brick building was 20 by 30 feet with an adjoining walled exercise yard. Presently, the gaol has three rooms on the first floor, a large one for the gaoler and two smaller ones for male and female prisoners. Attic chambers were used to confine petty offenders.

Gaol keepers were poorly paid — the original salary was a mere 30 pounds a year — consequently they possibly took out their frustrations on the hapless prisoners. Oddly, the keeper was also under orders to take prisoners condemned to death to Bruton Parish Church every Sunday until their execution date, "to make their prayers."

And it wasn't just convicted murderers who received the death sentence in colonial Williamsburg. Hanging was often the penalty for arson, piracy, horse stealing, forgery, and stealing. Once three men were hanged for stealing some clothes from a clergyman's house. If one escaped the noose, he was sometimes branded with an "'M" on his hand, for murder, or a "T" for thievery.

The Gaol

Writing in the Virginia Magazine of History and Biography in January 1964, Hugh F. Rankin described what happened on execution day. "Around noon of the day specified in the death warrant, the condemned man was taken from the jail. Placed on a cart, and attended by a clergyman, he was drawn to the 'public gallows, near this city.' The sheriff, in his capacity as public hangman, was waiting. The cart was pulled into place beneath the gallows. In the 'hush' that fell over the crowd of onlookers, the condemned man was allowed to speak his last words.

"At the completion of these final remarks, the doomed man, noose snug around his neck, was 'turn'd off' the cart."

Rankin noted that not all men died easily. When it came time to hang Anthony Francis Dittond, the confessed slayer of Mr. Evans, the coachmaker, Dittond "strugged after two or three minutes of swinging at the end of the rope. The executioner then grasped his legs and bore down to strangle him 'and put him out of his Pain the sooner'." But instead, the rope broke and both men fell to the ground. Dittond lay motionless for a few minutes, then recovered, got back up, asked the crowd "heartily to pray for him," climbed back onto the cart and was hanged a second time!

Rankin added that women convicted of felonies "departed this life beneath the same gallows as did male criminals."

At times, after the hangings, the prisoners' bodies were strung up for public viewing as a warning to the populace. This happened sometime around 1720 to four pirates who had threatened to have "vented their imprecations on their Judges and all concerned in their prosecution, and vow'd if they were at liberty they would spare none alive that should fall into their hands."

In this instance, Governor Spotswood felt that an "unusually severe punishment was justified." After being executed, two of the pirates were hanged in chains at Tindall's Point on the York River, and two were similarly strung up at Urbanna on the Rappahannock River. (Cause for a vengeful ghost to return?)

There was also, for a time, a quaint and highly unpleasant custom involving the men who served on the coroner's jury. They were required to literally view the victim's body. And if the victim happened to have been buried in the time between the crime, the capture of the murderer, and his subsequent trial, the body had to be exhumed so the jurors could view it.

Such was the system of justice in colonial times. The gaol served the colony until 1780, and was used as a jail by the city of Williamsburg until 1910.

Visitors today can only imagine the deplorable conditions which existed more than two centuries ago. Thus one might well suspect that ghostly moans from those about to be executed, or maniacal shrieks from the crazed and tortured, would reverberate in the night air surrounding the gaol. Yet, there have been no such reports at the site.

Still, there have been some inexplicable sounds. Some years ago, an historical interpreter, who has asked to remain nameless, was in the gaol early one morning, preparing to open the building to tourists for the day. No one else was around.

Suddenly, she heard sounds from the floor above her. She described it as appearing to be two women in high heeled shoes walking back and forth across the floor. And they seemed to be talking. The interpreter clearly heard them, although she couldn't quite make out what they were saying. The upstairs rooms often had been used as living quarters for jailers in past years. Curious, the interpreter went upstairs to look.

There was no one there!

CHAPTER 5

The Legend of Lady Skipwith – Part II

(Author's note: The first "Ghosts of Williamsburg" included a chapter on the ghost of Lady Ann Skipwith, who allegedly is heard clopping up the staircase late at night in the Wythe House in Colonial Williamsburg just down the green from the Palace. She is heard clopping because, according to long-standing tradition, she went to a ball at the Palace 200 or so years ago, became miffed at her husband, Peyton Skipwith, and raced back to the Wythe House where she was staying at the time. Along the way she lost one of her high-heeled red slippers, and thus, as she ascended the stairs it sounded almost like someone going up with a peg leg.)

The house itself is named for George Wythe (rhymes with Smith), one of our most under-publicized founding fathers. A brilliant scholar, he was admitted to the bar at the tender age of 20. When he married Elizabeth Taliaferro in 1755, her father gave her the handsome brick residence, of which the Virginia Landmarks Register has said: "The complex geometry of its proportions, combined with its subtle brickwork, demonstrate how Virginia's otherwise plain colonial architecture could transcend provinciality and achieve stateliness."

Wythe's credentials in more than 50 years service in Virginia, as a lawyer, professor of law, legislator, and judge, are as impressive as many of his more-famous students, including Thomas

Wythe House

Jefferson, James Monroe and John Marshall. Among other accomplishments, he was the first professor of law (at the College of William and Mary) in the country; he was the first Virginian to sign the Declaration of Independence; he designed the distinctive seal of the Commonwealth of Virginia; he was a delegate to both the first and second Continental Congresses; and he served as speaker of the House of Delegates in 1777.

Jefferson referred to Wythe as "my faithful and beloved Mentor in youth, and my most affectionate friend through life." He called Wythe, "One of the greatest men of the age, always distinguished by the most spotless virtue."

In 1791, Wythe moved from his house in Williamsburg to Richmond to become chancellor of Virginia. He died a tragic death in 1806 after being poisoned by his grandnephew, George Sweeney. In desperate financial straits, Sweeney, as the principal beneficiary of Wythe's will, hoped to gain his inheritance. But the wily Wythe, nearly 80 years old, lingered in agony for two weeks before dying — long enough for him to disinherit Sweeney. Ironically, the grandnephew was never convicted of the crime, primarily because the testimony of a slave, who had witnessed the act, was not then admissible in Virginia courts.

When I first published "The Ghosts of Williamsburg," in 1983, I said at the time, "there are no reported hauntings of Wythe's spirit in Williamsburg."

I stand corrected.

There are at least two published accounts of George Wythe's ghost. In "Romantic and Historic Virginia," (1935) author A. Hyatt Verrill contends that the house not only is haunted, but is "most thoroughly and completely haunted at that!" And by as many as three spirits!

Here is what he wrote: "The first of these wraiths is, so it is generally believed, the restless spirit of Judge Wythe himself, who was murdered in Richmond, and who, perhaps, resents strangers sleeping in his former bedroom. At all events, whoever sleeps in the Judge's chamber on the night of the Eighth of June, is certain to be awakened by the terrifying touch of a cold and clammy hand upon his brow.

"As far as I have been able to ascertain, no person who has slept in the haunted room has ever actually seen the ghost, hence it is merely supposition that it is the spirit of the worthy professor and judge. Moreover, although the phantom is credited with being a dangerous and aggressive ghost, I have found no evidence that it has ever actually harmed anyone, and it would seem entirely out of keeping with Judge Wythe's character and profession in life for his ghost to inflict bodily harm upon a person. . . Far more probably the Judge's ghost is merely lonely and desires to have a friendly midnight chat with the occupant of his one-time bedroom."

The author continues: "Although there is some reason for the ghost of Judge Wythe to haunt the old homestead — for it is a well known fact that the spirits of murdered men are ever restless — there seems to be no explanation for the presence of the other two ghosts who frequent the house. There is no question as to their identity, and the apparition that has been seen many a time walking back and forth in the wide hallway is unmistakable. Clearly visible in the moonlight filtering in through the small-paned windows, is the ghost of no less a personage that George Washington, powdered wig, regimental uniform, high boots and all. As I have said, it is a mystery as to why the spirit of Washington should haunt the Wythe House."

(It should be noted here that in 1781, Washington did, in fact, use the house as his headquarters during the planning for the siege of Yorktown, which led to the conclusion of the Revolutionary War.)

The third ghost the author mentions is, of course, Lady Ann Skipwith.

The presence of George Wythe's spectral return is also covered in William Oliver Stevens" 1938 book, "Old Williamsburg." He wrote: "Unhappily, Chancellor Wythe was poisoned by a villainous nephew to whom he had bequeathed a large amount of his estate. The murder was committed in Richmond, but the old gentleman's ghost came back to haunt his old house in Williamsburg where it felt more at home.

"Regularly, on the eighth of June, the anniversary of his murder, George Wythe emerges from the closet of his bedroom and lays a chilly hand of the face of whoever is sleeping therein.

"There is a story that the subsequent owner, instead of being disturbed by this ghostly tenant, used the room for his unwelcome guests. He contrived to invite them to come for the first fortnight in June. They never tarried after the morning of June 9, and never returned." (Stevens added that this owner used this tactic after a maiden aunt, invited for perhaps a week, decided to stay 30 years!)

Stevens also tells of Lady Ann's ghostly visitations, and even adds the possible occasional presence of yet another haunt. "A third ghost is Governor John Page, who bought the Wythe House for his home and who liked it so well that he still prefers it to the Elysian Fields, or whatever other place his spirit occupies. Apparently, he does nothing in particular but loaf about. He wasn't very picturesque. As he never had a broken heart and wasn't murdered, his spirit behaves in a quiet, well-bred way."

And finally there is this. The predominant legend at Wythe House continues to be the spectral presence of Lady Ann Skipwith. In 1994, I got a phone call from a young lady in Seattle, Washington, named Vickie Galloway. She told me she and a friend had taken the nightly Williamsburg ghost tour in May 1994 during a vacation, and she was so enamored with Lady Ann that she decided to visit the house the next day.

She took a photograph of the stairway inside the house, which Ann clopped up one shoe on and one off. Very excitedly, Vickie then told me that when she had the photos processed, <u>Lady Skipwith's apparition appeared on the stairs!</u> Would I be interested in seeing a copy of the print she asked. Would I?!!!

Here is the photo she sent. In her letter, Vickie said she and her friend toured Wythe House May 19, 1994. "I took pictures to illustrate the story of Lady Ann for anyone who would listen to my vacation travelog," she wrote. "As a last thought, I took the

enclosed photo looking down the stairs from the upstairs landing. When I got the pictures back from the developer, there was Lady Ann! In case anyone asks, I was using 100 ASA, Fuji film and a Ricoh point and shoot 35 mm camera. She had both her film and camera checked and they were in fine working order.

"I'm really anxious to hear your reaction to my photo. Both Carol (her friend) and I have become very fond of her."

I have to admit it is one of the most fascinating photos I have seen. Is it the apparition of Lady Ann? Or could it be George Wythe or one of the other phantoms? Since she took the photo in May and Wythe himself was said only to appear on the eighth of June, I tend to lean towards it being a female entity. Judge for yourself.)

CHAPTER 6

The Mystery Lady of the Ghost Tour

(Author's note: One of the things that continually astounds me is the ever-growing popularity of the public interest in ghost lore and legends. When I began writing about this subject in 1982 there was a general reluctance among those who had experienced paranormal activity to even discuss their encounters. They thought people would think them crazy. As more of my books came out and these "spectral witnesses" saw that others had felt similar "presences," they became more open.)

Similarly, in 1982 most hotels, bed and breakfasts, inns, and restaurants absolutely refused to admit anything in their establishments of a supernatural flavor. Today, these owners now candidly promote their resident ghosts. It has become a sort of haunting marketing tool.

And, over the past several years, a spooky cottage industry has sprung up from nowhere. Today, in Virginia alone, there are literally dozens of ghost tours offered. Some are held on or around Halloween. Some are nightly.

Now, what if you take such a tour, expecting perhaps to get goose bumps if you believe, or scoff if you don't believe — and you see something ethereal yourself! Wouldn't that be a kick? Well, that's exactly what happened to a lady from Fairfax, Virginia, named Kathy Heer. Here is what she wrote me:

"My husband and I were in Williamsburg March 26-28th

(1998) for a little get away while grandma watched our two kids. We did not have ghosts on our minds, but we had an eerie experience that you might be interested in.

"We made a reservation to go on the ghost walk tour. The weather was balmy, warm, and it was a beautiful night. An older woman was our guide. About three-quarters into the tour my husband and I were standing on the outer perimeter of the group listening to the guide. I remember we were standing at the end of a tall boxwood hedge that the guide pointed out as being 200 years old. She had just told us about the house where the first Christmas tree in America was erected. Our tour group was all alone on the street at this point.

"Suddenly my husband nudged me and said, 'Look at that statue,' and pointed to a spot on the side of the Christmas tree house in the shadows on the edge of a pale circle of light put off by a flood light high in a tree. I saw a small woman all dressed in black, her dark hair in a bun, with her arms crossed underneath a shawl. Her face was unusually pale. As we stood mesmerized, she moved one pale arm from under her shawl, and put her hand on her cheek, as if worried.

"She was looking off into the distance, not seeming to notice our group in the street off to the left of her. The rest of the tour group had their backs to her. The hair was standing up on the back of our necks as we stared at this strange figure for what seemed like a few minutes, but probably wasn't.

"Suddenly, she just faded into the shadows!

"My husband and I turned back to the group but no one else seemed to have noticed anything. We didn't know what to think. My first thought was that we'd seen some sort of prop for the ghost walk, and I kept waiting for the guide to say something about the woman in black. What she did talk about next was the woman in white appearing at the foot of a bed in the house next door to the one where we had seen our lady. (The Peyton Randolph House in Colonial Williamsburg).

"My husband and I did not talk about it until we were back in our car. Our shared opinion was that it had really been very strange, and why would a young woman wearing what appeared to be Civil War-era clothes be standing there at nine o'clock at night? If someone wanted to scare the tourists on the ghost walk, why didn't they do something more to attract attention?

"The scariest thing came out a little later when my husband, who works for the National Imagery and Mapping Agency, and analyzes photos and images from satellites, pointed out that while the evening was breezy and the trees were moving gently, and our guide had to continually push her hair out of her eyes, nothing was moving on the woman. Her hair was in a bun , but her skirt was full and her shawl appeared to be fringed. The breeze was moving nothing on her. I would never have picked up such an inconsistency but my husband has a trained eye.

"We are not assuming that this was anything supernatural, but it has given us pause. We are still talking about it. . . . I know this sounds a little crazy, to have taken place while on a ghost walk, but we are credible people and the occurrence seemed very odd to us. I've never seen anything that struck me so eerily. I am a psychologist by profession and well grounded in science but I do believe there are things we cannot explain. Did we have one of those experiences in Williamsburg? I truly wonder."

(The ghost tour people from Maximum Guided Tours say they know nothing of such a woman in black!)

C H A P T E R 7

The Missing Vault at Bruton Parish Church

o mystic spirits haunt the old cemetery at historic Bruton Parish Church in Williamsburg?

If not, then how else would one explain the unbelievably bizarre activities which took place in this otherwise quiet community in the summer and fall of 1991; events which shook townspeople to their core for a period of several months and created international media attention.

The strangeness seemed to peak in the early morning hours of November 27, 1991, when a Colonial Williamsburg security officer, patrolling the famous Duke of Gloucester Street at 4:30 in the morning, heard some noise coming from the Bruton Parish Church graveyard. He then shined his flashlight on an eerie scene: two men, pick and shovels in hand, were digging a huge hole amidst the centuries-old tombstones. The instant the beam of light hit them, the men dropped their tools, leaped over a brick wall, and escaped in the darkness. The officer then walked to the site of their activity and stared into the bottom of a seven-and-a-half-foot deep pit!

The mystery was not quite as deep as the pit, however, because this was the second attempt at an illegal entry into the sacred grounds of the church in two months. A previous surreptitious excavation had taken place during the pre-dawn hours of September 9, and it, too, had been interrupted by authorities. The perpetrators were then identified as being a trio of New Age

Bruton Parish Church

activists from Santa Fe, New Mexico: 39-year-old Marsha Middleton, her husband, Frank Flint, and Doug Moore.

They were not your everyday ordinary grave robbers. Quite the contrary. They were driven in their nocturnal quests by a profound belief that a secret vault lay buried deep in a corner of the cemetery — a vault which they felt held invaluable papers that would provide the guidance to a "new world order." So possessed were they in their quest to uncover the subterranean vault, that even after they had been caught and identified in the September dig, and threatened with prosecution if they ever returned, they came back to search again in November anyway. Mrs. Middleton said at the time that they "were guided" to come back by a Biblical passage in the book of Revelations: "We have to stand up for what we believe and know is true."

What they believed was that the mystical vault, which they said was buried secretly in early colonial days, contained copper cylinders holding the lost manuscripts of Sir Francis Bacon, a brilliant philosopher and scientist who was born in England in 1561 and died in 1626. Further, these papers were said to hold the key for a "new united world, and would be a precursor to the second coming of Jesus Christ." It was also speculated that the manuscripts would prove that Bacon was actually the author of the great works that have been attributed to William Shakespeare!

Such an extraordinary assertion was not new with Mrs. Middleton and her tunneling associates. In fact, the feeling that such a vault existed was first raised more than 60 years ago by a California woman named Marie Bauer Hall. She had done extensive research on the subject and came to Williamsburg in 1938 to sponsor an authorized search at Bruton Parish Church.

Mrs. Hall became convinced that Bacon's long-lost manuscripts had not really been lost at all — they had been hidden. She said that by deciphering complex codes contained in Bacon's published works, in Shakespeare's plays, and on ancient church tombstones, she had discovered that one of Bacon's descendants had brought the invaluable papers to America and buried them at the Williamsburg site in 1676.

The current church was built in 1715, but a previous church existed there before, dating into the 17th century. Armed with her research studies and properly financed, Mrs. Hall somehow convinced vestry officials to allow her to dig for the vault. Excavations began on June 9, 1938, at the base of the bell tower. At a depth of nine feet, workers came upon a "tomb-like structure." Mrs. Hall said this was not the vault, and that they had been digging in the wrong place. She then began to decipher directions from other tombstones in the cemetery, and felt the actual location would be nearer the site of the original church foundation.

Records indicated the first building had been completed in 1683. By translating dates on the stones into feet she determined where they should next dig. For example, one grave marker date of 1711 was measured off at 1,711 feet from a point on the nearby

College of William and Mary campus, which she said she had decoded as being the point from which to start.

On August 26, 1938, they began again, and this time they uncovered "bricks laid in the form of an old foundation." Three days later the entire foundation was laid bare, 65 feet by 28 feet, which is exactly what Mrs. Hall had predicted. The dig stirred considerable excitement in the then-sleepy town. College students and visitors crowded the scene and created a circus-like atmosphere. Eventually, at a depth of nearly 20 feet, "a body of about 10 feet square, partially filled and much larger than an ordinary tomb," was found.

At this point, for a reason that remains unexplained to this day, church officials abruptly ordered the massive hole filled. Mrs. Hall said she was never told why the effort was discontinued. So the mystery remained unsolved, and largely forgotten, for nearly 50 years.

In 1985, Mrs. Hall, who apparently had never lost faith in her belief that the vault existed, arranged for some scientific testing at the site. This included ground penetrating radar, magneto metric readings and electrical resistivity measurements. The first results were unsuccessful because they didn't go deep enough. However, subsequent tests turned up tantalizing clues. One of the investigators, Dr. Billy Hibbard, a chemist, said, "Absolutely, there is a chance something is there because we got a basic difference in resistance measurements in the area they believe the vault is located."

Again, strangely, the testing was halted, and the parish grounds were left undisturbed until Mrs. Middleton and the two men arrived on the scene in 1991. Amidst a swirl of publicity generated by their two nocturnal diggings, church officials finally relented and authorized a team of Colonial Williamsburg archeological experts and a geology professor to try and answer once and for all the question of whether or not there was a vault there.

In the summer of 1992 they began work, drilling core borings straight down and at diagonal angles under the grave site of Anna Graham. They again found the foundations of the original church, and a portion of a casket made of wood with straps of leather around it. This was believed to be the grave of a child. The experts drilled deeply into the ground and said they found only soil which had been "undisturbed for thousands of years."

This seemed to satisfy all but the most die-hard Bacon enthusiasts, including Mrs. Middleton and her team. They still believed the vault existed somewhere in the Bruton Parish church yard, and that the archeologists had bored in the wrong place.

And so, to some at least, the mystery remains. Is there a vault? Does it contain the missing Bacon papers? Would such papers prove that Bacon had written Shakespeare's plays? Would the papers also lay the groundwork for a New World Order?

Such puzzlers may never be answered. There are a couple of intriguing footnotes to this whole incredible episode, one psychically related. Ivor Noel Hume is the much respected, retired head of archeology at Colonial Williamsburg. He is an expert of international renown, and has written a number of books and articles on colonial era discoveries. At the height of the controversy, in October 1991, at a public meeting on the subject of the vault, he told a crowd of townspeople, curiosity seekers, and media representatives that he had in his possession a tape of a psychic reading made in Canada in 1974. The reading indicated that a "mysterious vault" was buried in a churchyard. The psychic said it contained "a box with maps and papers," and she identified the owner of the box as . . . Sir Francis Bacon!

And then, one wonders why church authorities so abruptly halted the 1938 excavations, just when it appeared they were about to discover something which might unveil the mystery. One of those who questioned this peculiar action is Marshall Allen, a retired mechanical engineer now living in Pennsylvania. He had been a student at William and Mary in 1938, and had witnessed the diggings then. He was interviewed by Richmond Times Dispatch writer Wilford Kale in September 1991. Kale wrote that "something was found about 10 feet under the Bruton Parish Church yard in November 1938. Some people said it was a burial vault. Indeed, church vestry minutes cryptically suggested it was a coffin."

Allen disagreed. "It looked too wide to be a coffin," he said. Kale noted that Allen "believes something was found that caused either Bruton vestry leaders or Colonial Williamsburg officials to suddenly end the excavations." Allen added that "had the vault ever been buried on the site it would have been easy to find by digging down to the undisturbed earth, but in the manner in which it was performed, there can be no conclusive evidence given.

"I know they found a very large box," Allen continued. "It was about four-and-a-half feet wide and they didn't know how long it was because it was never uncovered. They never finished digging it out. It was between nine and 10 feet deep. . . When the box was found, photographers climbed over the wall and jumped inside of the hole and began taking pictures. Everyone got excited and they (the officials) cleared out the whole mess. Then the church people said that's a coffin and we can't have any more digging and everything was stopped. They could have found out what it was. But the way it was handled left a bad taste and is the reason why the story has continued until this day."

It thus seems somehow appropriate that a nightly ghost tour winds up at the Bruton Parish Church cemetery. There, tourists are told of some of the legendary haunts of the area, unaware that they are standing near sacred grounds that may contain the answer to one of the most enigmatic mysteries of all!

* * * * * *

THE MYSTICAL NEW AGE

New Age religion has been described as encompassing a myriad of beliefs, which, for the most part, deal with the mystical side of religion, ranging from pyramid power and astrology to out-of-body experiences. It is said to be a religion "with a vision" to create a "new world order" that would allow drawing on other unusual beliefs for the development of personal faith. Mrs. Hall's late husband, Manly P. Hall, was reported to be one of the founders of New Age, and the Los Angeles Times once called him, before his death in 1990, "the last remaining Western mystic." Many New Agers believed that Sir Francis Bacon set a course for the new world order in the papers he wrote; papers that have been missing for nearly four centuries.

CHAPTER 8

The Mystery Surrounding Matthew Whaley's Death

There is one tombstone in the cemetery next to historic Bruton Parish Church which seems to attract more than its share of small visitors. Children almost appear drawn to the grave of little Matthew Whaley, who was born in 1696. He died when he was but nine years old.

The inscription on the tomb reads: "MATTHEW WHALEY lyes Interred here Within This Tomb upon his Father dear, Who Departed This Life the 26th of September 1705, Aged Nine years, only child of JAMES WHALEY and MARY, his wife."

There also is an enduring aura of mystery surrounding this young lad. First, it appears uncertain as to just how he died. There are at least three versions. Whichever way he passed on, it was well before "his time."

Consequently, persistent reports have circulated over the past 50 years or so that the elementary school in Williamsburg which bears his name is haunted with Matthew's spirit. A number of teachers and students there have told of unexplained footsteps and other noises in the hallways and certain classrooms which are supposed to be empty. All searches have proven futile. There also have been a few rare glimpses of the apparition of a small boy wandering through the school.

Matthew's mother, Mary Page Whaley, was a school teacher in the colonial capital. She returned to England after her only son's death and when she died in 1742, she donated property and money to build a school in his honor. It is adjacent to the Governor's Palace.

Tomb of Matthew Whaley

Historian and author Lyon G. Tyler, the son of President John Tyler, wrote about Matthew and his mother in his book, "Williamsburg, The Old Colonial Capital," published in 1907. "There is now standing on the site of the palace a brick structure erected in 1867 out of the money left for a free school by Mrs. Mary Whaley. . . The story of this benefaction is romantic. After the collapse of Bacon's rebellion, in 1676, Richard Lawrence, Thomas Whaley and John Forth, three of Bacon's friends, fled to the woods 'in snow ankle deep,' and were never heard of again.

"But Thomas Whaley left in York County a son, James Whaley, who became a prominent merchant and justice of the peace. He married Mary Page, daughter of Matthew Page and niece of Colonel John Page. They had an only son, Matthew, who died while a child. "Therefore, 'to eternalize Mattey's name forever,' as she expressed it in her will, Mrs. Whaley established a free school on the east side of Queen Mary's road, leading to the capitol land-ing, very near the present railroad bridge. Mrs. Whaley's buildings consisted of a school house, the master's house, and a stable. She removed to London, and, in 1742, died there leaving a considerable legacy to her school."

Tyler goes on to say that legal wranglings over Mrs. Whaley's estate caused a delay of the funds for the school — for more than 100 years! It was not until 1867, that the money finally arrived in Virginia (cause enough for a ghostly return?) Tyler said authorities used most of the fund, now swelled by interest to several thousand pounds, to "erect upon the site of the palace the brick house men-tioned, and in it they now maintain 'The Matthew Whaley Observation and Practice School."

In November 1995, students at the school celebrated a Matthew Whaley day, complete with ox cart rides, performances by a fife and drum corps, and balladeers, and a feast of Brunswick stew and spoon bread. No one reported seeing or hearing Matthew that day, but some said they felt an eerie sort of "presence," as if they were being watched by unseen eyes.

Exactly how Matthew departed this earth, however, remains shrouded in mystery to this day. Some believe he died of pneumo-nia. Others have heard the cause of his death was accidental; that he fell off a horse. And, finally, there is an article in an old Tyler's Quarterly Historic Magazine which stated that he "returned to England to finish his education and make the grand tour of Europe, which, after having done with great credit and improve-ment, he set sail for Virginia in a vessel, which foundered at sea and every soul on board perished."

Whatever happened, it appears that young Mattey returns on occasion to visit the school named for him, and enjoy the compan-ionship of his peers which he missed in life.

CHAPTER 9

The Apparitional Return of Cuthbert Ogle

lthough the history of 18th century Virginia is more than well documented in the Colonial Williamsburg Foundation library, the Swem Library at the College of William and Mary, the state library in Richmond and elsewhere, relatively little is known about a poor, though apparently talented English musician who came to America probably in the late winter or early spring of 1755.

His name was Cuthbert Ogle.

It is recorded that on March 28th of that year, he ran an ad in the Virginia Gazette offering his services to teach "Gentlemen and Ladies to play on the Organ, Harpsichord or Spinet; and to instruct those Gentlemen that play on other instruments so as to enable them to play in Concert." He went on to say that he was living at the Nicolson house (circa 1752) in Williamsburg, but that "upon having Encouragement," he would be willing to "fix to any Part of the Country."

This could have indicated that he was having a rough time making ends meet, which was true of most musicians of that era. Peter Pelham, for example, the celebrated musician and organist at Bruton Parish Church from the 1750s to the 1790s, subsidized his meager earnings by serving as the town's jailer. There are sketchy, and unconfirmed, notes that suggest Ogle plied the plantation circuit briefly, playing and teaching music to the aristocratic set. And there are accounts that he was brought over to America not only to be the first organist at Bruton Parish, before Pelham, but also to help install the church's initial organ. Some writers have even called him an "outstanding" musician of the mid-18th century.

If indeed he did achieve a measure of fame, it was short-lived, because Cuthbert Ogle died on April 23, 1755, leaving a scant estate worth only 69 pounds, including such assorted items as a nightshirt, a spyglass, an old grey coat and two pairs of "breeches," two pairs of spectacles, a plain gold watch, a fiddle and a case, several "musick" books, two "wigs" and a hair trunk.

The word was that this mysterious musician passed away even before the organ could be assembled in the church. His legacy of a music library, the importance of which is difficult to ascertain, was allegedly passed on to young Pelham.

It is the ghost, or more precisely, the "presence" of Cuthbert Ogle that is felt in the Nicolson House on York Street, according to Cathy Short, who lived there from 1965 to 1980. "We always called him Cuthbert anyway," she says. Robert Nicolson was a tailor and merchant. His house was built around the middle of the 18th century. He took in lodgers for a number of years, and during the Revolutionary War he and his son, William, provided uniforms to the American army.

Nicolson House

"Of course, there are many noises physically associated with old houses," Cathy says, "and we certainly had our share of creaks and rattles and squeaky steps. But beyond this, there was a definite presence in the house. My husband and oldest son never really felt it, but my youngest son, David, and I often did. And it was a male. I can't tell you why I know this. It was an unstated feeling. At times you could just sense there was something there, always on the second floor. David and I would know this without conferring, yet it never bothered either one of us."

Once, Cathy had some friends over and they were playing bridge downstairs. One, the late Lee Epley, went upstairs to the bathroom, and when she came down, she had an astonished look on her face. "Do you know you have a ghost in this house?" she asked. Cathy, concentrating hard on her card game, didn't even look up. "Yeah," she said, matter of factly. "The other women couldn't believe how nonchalant I was," she adds.

On another occasion, Dot Rascoe of Williamsburg was in the house with others for a meeting when Cathy told them the story of Cuthbert. "I was sitting on the couch," Dot recalls, "and I felt something tap me on the shoulder. I thought it was the cat, but when I turned around, there was nothing there!" A similar, though less-than-supernatural occurrence happened one night when several college students were at the house. Again, Cathy was talking about the resident ghost, when her cat playfully tapped one of the coeds on the head. She screamed, and Cathy says, "You never saw so many young ladies move so fast."

Once, in the dead of the night, Cathy kept hearing scratching sounds. "I thought it might be a rat or a squirrel, but finally I couldn't stand it any longer. I woke my husband and told him there was someone in the room other than us. He turned on the light and looked around, but found nothing. He went back to bed and said, sarcastically, 'it must be Cuthbert.' Just then, inexplicably, the lamp on his bedside table fall to the floor. And it didn't just fall. It ended up all the way across the room, as if someone had thrown it there. After that, my husband thought maybe there was something to our ghost theory after all."

Reminiscences at the Raleigh Tavern

"**H**ilaritas Sapientiae et Bonae Vitae Proles" — ("Jollity is the child of wisdom and good living.") This is the motto which adorns historic Raleigh Tavern on Duke of Gloucester Street in Colonial Williamsburg. It sums up the philosophy and practice the Raleigh employed for more than 150 years of service as the most celebrated tavern in Virginia.

Established about 1717, the Raleigh was the Virginia colony's center of social, political and business activities. Historian Lyon G. Tyler, son of President John Tyler, wrote of the Raleigh nearly a century ago: "The Apollo was the main room in the tavern. It was well lit, having a deep fireplace, on each side of which a door opened, with carved wainscoting beneath the windows and above the mantelpiece." (It is believed the Apollo was named after the Apollo room in London's Devil's Tavern, a favorite haunt of Sir Walter Raleigh.)

Tyler added: "This room witnessed probably more scenes of brilliant festivity and political excitement than any other single apartment in North America." At least four governors — Spotswood, Gooch, Dinwiddie and Botetourt — supped here. "And with the advent of the Revolution, it grew suddenly popular as a meeting place for the patriots."

Why was the Raleigh so well liked? It probably was a combination of good food, spacious meeting rooms, amiable hosts, and a brilliant array of customers. And there is this: one of the first tavern keepers was Henry Wetherburn who is said to have invented

Raleigh Tavern

"arrack punch." Author William Oliver Stevens wrote, "So potent and beguiling was this concoction that one William Randolph of Tuckahoe (near Richmond) sold 200 acres of land to the father of Thomas Jefferson for the price of 'Henry Wetherburn's biggest bowl of Arrack punch'."

To this, Tyler adds, "(The Raleigh) had long been used for balls and assemblies, and, in 1764, we find (Thomas) Jefferson, then a gay young man studying in the law office of George Wythe, writing from 'Devilsburg,' as he called Williamsburg, that he was as happy on the night before as 'dancing with Belinda in the Apollo could make him.'

"This ancient room indeed saw, at one time or another, all that was brilliant and graceful in the Virginia society of the 18th century."

It was here at the Raleigh that some of America's most famous forefathers, in heated discussion and debate, began sowing the seeds for revolution. In February 1769, for example, after the English parliament advised the king to transport persons accused of treason in America for trial in Great Britain, the incensed burgesses of Virginia passed "warm resolutions" denouncing this. When then-Governor Lord Botetourt, upset at this action, dissolved the official assembly, the burgesses retired to the Apollo Room and proceeded there to adopt a "non-importation" agreement.

On June 1, 1774, the burgesses met at the Raleigh again and passed resolutions against the use of tea and other East India goods in protest of the British shutting down Boston Harbor following the famous "Tea Party."

The list of notables who partook of the fare and participated in the historic events at the Raleigh is unmatched.

— George Washington often noted in his diary that he dined here, and he was once given a surprise birthday party in the Apollo Room.

— Patrick Henry was honored at a farewell dinner hosted by his Virginia troops.

— Peyton Randolph was feted here after he came home from serving as president of the first Continental Congress.

— The Marquis de Lafayette was given an extravagant banquet in the Apollo Room during his triumphant return to Virginia in 1824.

Against such an illustrious background one might think the spirits of some legendary figures linger here. Not so. There have been a few scattered notations by passersby of hearing the sounds of a "party" taking place within the tavern's walls. And the pungent scent of pipe tobacco also has been sniffed. Queer, because no smoking has been allowed inside for years. There has been no plausible explanation for the sounds or the smells. Each time those who witnessed the phenomena looked in on darkened, empty rooms.

Perhaps the absence of any famous phantoms lies in the fact that the tavern burned to the ground in 1859. It was restored more than 70 years later.

And so one wonders what the original walls of the old Raleigh might have yielded had they not been consumed by fire. What magnificent conversations and testimonies, and ringing declarations of freedom they must have held!

A Sampling of
Spectral Vignettes

THE 'SEE-THROUGH' MAN AT TARPLEY'S STORE

One day several years ago, an English lady was working at Tarpley's Store in Colonial Williamsburg, a popular place of trade in the second half of the 18th century.

The lady went upstairs to a private area to check on some inventory and came face to face with a man nattily attired in colonial costume.

She said he was there, but he wasn't there, meaning he was an apparition. She could see through him!

She raced down the stairs and breathlessly told her supervisor what she had seen. Curiously, the supervisor said, "Oh no, you didn't see anything.!

* * * * *

RED EYES SHINING IN THE DARK

What would your reaction be if, sleeping late at night for the first time in a strange house, you woke up, and, peering straight out of the guest bedroom down the stairway to the ground floor, you saw a pair of red, flickering eyes staring at you? Fright? Horror? Would you scream? Likely.

Tarpley's Store

But Shiela Lake only stared back in fascination.

She still remembers the date—November 28, 1981. She and her husband, Dick, who now run a bed and breakfast in Williamsburg, were in town to check out the William and Mary campus for their oldest son. Rather than stay at a motel, they chose to spend the night in the small building behind Peter Hay's rebuilt apothecary shop, which, they felt, had more "atmosphere." After a late dinner at King's Arms Tavern, they sat before the fireplace until about midnight and then retired to the upstairs bedroom.

"You walk right into the bedroom from the stairs," Shiela recalls. "There is a landing halfway up the stairs and a shoulder high window is located there. Dick had fallen asleep, and I had the strangest sensation that I was being watched. I was lying on one side and when I turned over, I looked through the open door down the stairway. I saw these two red spots. At first, I thought it might be a reflection of the fire in the window, but then, as my eyes adjusted, I saw the distinct shape of a man. The red spots were his eyes!

"For some reason I can't explain, I wasn't frightened. Instinctively, I knew somehow that 'he' wouldn't harm me. I turned my head and then looked back again. He was still there. I could see the outline of him from his head down just above his ankles. He had on a kind of blouse that seemed to billow at his shoulders. His trousers were like knickers coming down to just below his knees, with long white socks under them. He didn't move, except for the flickering lights in his eyes. And his head seemed to be swathed in bandages.

"After awhile, I guess I nodded off," Shiela says. "Then I awoke again about 3 a.m., and I had to go to the bathroom. I turned on the night light and looked down the stairs. There was nothing there. Then, when I got back in bed and turned out the light, I looked again, and there he was, the red eyes glowing as before!"

In reading about the history of the area sometime later, Shiela gasped when she read where Peter Hay's shop had burned to the ground in 1756. Despite his head having been wrapped in bandages, Shiela had the impression that the vision she saw that night was that of a black man. Could it have been a servant, injured in the fire, who had come back to see who was sleeping in his quarters?

* * * * *

NIGHT NOISES IN THE TRAVIS HOUSE

 he Edward Travis House, built in 1765, later became the residence of superintendents of the public hospital, devoted exclusively to the care and treatment of the mentally ill.

An employee in the house some years ago said he was shaken by a series of loud noises of undetermined origin.

Alone, he looked through the building but found nothing. He said a glass ashtray then split in two, a filing cabinet began shaking violently, and the doors slammed shut.

He left the building abruptly.

* * * * *

MISS GIBBIE GALT'S SECRET ROOM

 hat is the secret behind Miss Gibbie Galt's mystery room?

Miss Gibbie, actually Miss Gabriella Galt, was a schoolteacher in Williamsburg generations ago. She lived in what has long been known as the old Stuart House.

It was furnished, top to bottom, with mahogany. Inside the front door stood a tall secretary with elaborate brass trimming. It was said to have once been owned by Lord Dunmore.

Like another lady of Williamsburg's past, Mad Lucy Ludwell ,Miss Gibbie was, well, sort of eccentric. She was described as being "not pretty," but she was so intellectually engaging, and possessed such "wit and vivacity," that she drew a cadre of admiring young men wherever she went.

Every weekday her home was filled with town children whom she scrupulously tutored. She was determined they would get a good education whether they liked it or not.

There was an air of mystery about the house, the sense of which seemed most acute on rainy days. Town rumor had it that some of Miss Gibbie's family members had met tragic deaths there.

One room upstairs had been closed off for years. It was said this room was haunted. Miss Gibbie added fuel to the speculation by saying only that "there was blood in that room and it must never be disturbed."

Some of the children swore they heard sighs and groans coming from beyond the locked door, and they said they saw blood trickling from beneath the door on occasions.

The dark secret of the mystery room was never solved. It was forever sealed with the death of Miss Gibbie many years ago.

* * * * *

A LOVING SPIRIT AT THE PALACE

(Author's note: In January 1993, I got a phone call from a woman named Sybil Parr, in Davie, Florida. "I have read your books, and I have had an experience that I just have to tell you," she said in an excited voice. She had been a travel agent, and had taken a tour of Colonial Williamsburg in 1984 with a group of other agents. During a visit to the Palace, she had been "overwhelmed" by a supernatural presence. Following is what she told me.)

 "s soon as I entered the building, some being of some kind wrapped around me. I don't

The Palace

know how to explain it. It was inside me, all over me. It enveloped me. I was warm all over. It was the best feeling I ever had. This spirit, or whatever it was, loved me. I knew that. It was a fabulous experience.

"I am distantly related to the Adams family, and I asked one of the guides if the Adams had ever come there. But I had the strong sensation that whoever it was, it knew me. It kept holding me, caressing me. It was such a loving, warm feeling. Afterwards, I had to go back to the hotel. I couldn't continue on the tour. I was too shaken. The spirit had completely encased me.

"It had to be someone from my past. Maybe I was its wife in a past life. It felt like a man. It was like a reunion. I'm a Roman Catholic and I had never believed in reincarnation before, but I don't know how else to explain it. It loved me. The feeling lasted the whole time I was in the Palace, about 45 minutes. I never told anyone before. I thought they would think I was crazy, but I had to tell someone. I believe the spirit is still there. I hope to go back someday and see."

* * * * *

STRIPPED BEDS IN THE LIGHTFOOT HOUSE

This elegant two-story brick building, constructed in 1730, today is used to house distinguished guests who visit Colonial Williamsburg, such as foreign heads of state. The maids who service this house sometimes have a difficult time. On more than one occasion, for instance, they have freshly made up beds in a bedroom, only to turn around a few seconds later and see the bed stripped!

Lightfoot House

One cleaning lady said she saw a gentleman dressed in colonial costume there once. This is not an uncommon occurrence, because many foundation employees dress in 18th century clothing to lend period atmosphere. But this lady said what she saw was definitely not a mortal being. She was so spooked, in fact, that she quit on the spot!

* * * * *

A CURIOUS 'CROWD' AT THE CAPITOL

he original Capitol building in Colonial Williamsburg was completed in 1705, and was gutted by fire in 1747. A second structure, using the original "naked brick walls," was erected in 1753. After the removal of Virginia's government to Richmond in 1780, this capitol fell into disrepair, and it, too, was destroyed by fire in 1832. Colonial Williamsburg has restored it to its initial elegance.

Much of America's early history is tied to this site.

** It was here that Patrick Henry fanned the flames of revolution in 1765 with his fiery speech against the stamp act. One may recall that famous line he thundered: "If this be treason, make the most of it."

** It was here, on May 15, 1776, that the convention of Virginia called on Congress to declare the colonies free and independent states—an action that led directly to the Declaration of Independence.

Today, the British flag flies over the capitol. That's because it was a colonial capitol.

Could this somehow stir the spirits of patriots past? Perhaps.

In his 1938 book, "Old Williamsburg," William Oliver Stevens wrote: "They say that the portrait of Patrick Henry now in the capitol was quite pleasant-looking when it was first acquired . . . but that its present sour aspect of disgust and rage is due to that banner which flies over his head all day."

Stevens added: "Some Williamsburg inhabitants go so far as to say that on the stroke of midnight on every Fourth of July there is an assemblage of Revolutionary ghosts with Patrick Henry at their head who stand in front of the capitol and use most reprehensible language!"

The Capitol

* * * * *

A PAIR OF GHOSTLY BABYSITTERS

(Author's note: At a ghost talk I gave to the faculty at Clara Byrd Baker Elementary School a teacher named Linda Woodard came up to me afterwards and related the following experience:)

few years earlier, Linda and her husband had lived in a dependency building adjacent to the famous Bassett Hall in Colonial Williamsburg. Bassett Hall is the magnificent mansion in which John D. Rockefeller, Jr., lived when he came to Williamsburg to supervise the restoration of the colonial area, which he had endowed.

The Woodards had a 14-month-old child. The infant toppled out of its crib one day, but was not harmed.

Shortly after this, Linda came into the child's room one afternoon to check on it, and suddenly was paralyzed with fear. She clearly saw an apparitional woman leaning over the crib. The woman appeared to be quite elderly. Before she could react, Linda said, the woman dematerialized before her eyes.

Later, Linda again approached the room and saw another "old lady" bending over the crib. This woman was different, and, according to Linda, appeared to be "covered in ivy!" Again, this woman evaporated before her eyes.

"Somehow, I felt as if these two ladies were checking on my baby to make sure it didn't fall out of the crib again," Linda says. "I just had that feeling. They didn't appear threatening or to be harmful in any way. I wasn't really afraid of them, although I must admit it was pretty unsettling."

Sometime afterward, Linda learned, to her astonishment, that two ladies, matching the description of the figures she had seen, had, in fact, lived in the same dependency building decades before, but both had died long ago!

Were they indeed there to check on the child?

You can't convince Linda Woodard otherwise.

* * * * *

WHAT SECRETS LURK IN THE WILLIAMSBURG INN?

O f all the buildings in Colonial Williamsburg — the originals and the restored, some dating to the 17th century — one might theorize the one least expected to be haunted would be the Williamsburg Inn. After all, it did not exist in colonial times. It was, rather, constructed in the 1930s, and has since served as one of the finest hostelries in the nation. Its guests have included several U.S. Presidents and more foreign dignitaries than there is space to list.

Yet there are a couple of things that might give one pause.

A few years ago, the author got a call from a lady in Green Acres, Florida, named Esamel Payne. She told of a very chilling experience she had at the inn in 1970. She was in town then for a conference. The inn was full so she was given a room in an adjacent cabin. She couldn't sleep because of noise upstairs, so she called the desk, and somehow they found a room for her in the inn.

"I noticed that the bellman looked at me with a peculiar expression on his face when he showed me the room," she recalls. "I didn't think anything about it at the time. I fell asleep, but I was awakened around midnight when I heard the click of a key in the door and then heavy footsteps across the room. I turned on the light but there was no one there.

"I went back to sleep but was aroused again around 2:30 in the morning. I had the sensation that some 'little hands' were encircled around my neck and were choking me. It was quite unsettling. Again, I turned the light on but saw nothing. This time I had difficulty going back to sleep.

"Then, about six a.m. I heard screaming in the room. I was afraid to open my eyes. I got up. I went to my conference and came back to check out at about 5 p.m. Again, the bellhop had the strangest look, as if he couldn't wait to get out of that room. It was like he knew something evil had happened there. He looked scared. I somehow had the sense they maybe someone had been murdered in that room. I know this. It all wasn't a figment of my imagination."

(Author's note: Some years later I was told that there was a ghost photo on file at the Inn. Cathy Clark, an employee, said a guest had once taken a photo which clearly showed an apparitional figure on it. She had kept the photo in a file behind the front desk. But when I went to see it, the picture had mysteriously disappeared.)

* * * * *

THE 'BARREL MAN' OF THE BLUEBELL TAVERN

Of all the historic taverns in Colonial Williamsburg, the Bluebell had by far the worst reputation. Its seediness was exceeded only by the character

Bluebell Tavern

of its clientele, which included gruff-looking sailors on leave, disreputable characters, and other transients who could afford nothing else for food, ale, or lodging. In 1771, the owner was informed that his tavern was in "bad repair always rented to bad tenants, always nasty and few rents paid."

In the 18th century, many goods were stored behind the Bluebell, including hogsheads of supplies. Several current employees have reported seeing the wispy figure of a man in soiled clothes of colonial times, pushing a hogshead around the tavern in the moonlight.

* * * * *

THE HOUSE WHERE TIME STOOD STILL

Some years ago, Russell Simons moved into a boarding house on Lafayette Street in Williamsburg with the intent of finding a job in the colonial town. Simons was sound asleep one night when something suddenly woke him. When he opened his eyes he saw what he described as an apparitional woman standing about 10 feet from his bed. It was a smallish woman with dark hair and a "kindly face." He said she was staring at him and appeared to be "floating" a few inches above the floor. He added that the figure seemed to be transparent, because he could see, by moonlight streaming through a window, the window frame and curtains through the apparition.

While most people would be terrified at such a sight, Simons said he inexplicably felt completely at peace, and had the strong impression that the woman meant no harm to him. In fact, he went back to sleep, although he emphasized that he definitely was not asleep when the vision appeared to him.

The next morning when he awoke, he noticed that his electric alarm clock had stopped during the night, and he could not get it to start running again. Later, when he mentioned to his landlord that the clock had stopped and he needed to purchase another one, the man said not to waste his money.

The landlord then told him that when his wife had died, every clock in the house except one had stopped at the precise moment of her death. He told Simons that he had gone out and bought some new clocks, but they had all stopped, too. He then opened a desk drawer and showed Simons several clocks. They had all stopped at the same time as Simons had. The landlord then pointed to a very old clock hanging over the mantel. He said it was more than 150 years old and had been in his wife's family for generations. For some unknown reason, this was the only clock which would work in the house.

Also in the room was an old photograph of a woman. The landlord said it was a picture of his wife. Simons was astounded! It was the same woman he had seen in apparitional form in his room! Simons had been sleeping in her room.

Simons stayed in the house for a few more days and then moved into new quarters. He plugged in his alarm clock. It worked perfectly!

CHAPTER 12

The Stage Struck Specter at William and Mary

Every theater of note seems to have, or perhaps should have, a resident ghost, and Phi Beta Kappa Hall on the campus of the College of William and Mary in Williamsburg is no exception. Here, amidst the presentation of plays ranging from modern drama to Shakespeare, occasionally roams a spectral lady who students long ago named "Lucinda." She has been seen and heard, mostly in the lighting booth or around the stage manager's box for at least the past 40 years. For example:

— Thirty years ago music student Larry Raikin was by himself in the hall late one night practicing on the piano. Finished, he gathered his belongings and started to leave. Suddenly, a female voice materialized and said, "Oh, don't stop." Raikin looked all around only to find he was alone. He searched the entire auditorium, turning on all the lights he could find. When he entered the scene room below the stage, a fuse blew and the door slammed behind him, leaving him in total darkness for about 20 minutes. Terrified, he ran from the building.

— In 1970, following a concert at Phi Beta Kappa Hall, Raikin and Calvin Remsberg stayed to clean up. Late at night, they decided to improvise an opera with Raikin at the piano. Remsberg let out a cry of alarm as he saw "the figure of a woman dressed in a long black dress and black veil drift from the stage manager's box to the other side of the stage."

— Student Wayne Aycock opened a door one evening while

PhiBeta Kappa Hall

working in the lowered pit of the theater. As he did, sparks flew. He then heard organ music, and discovered, in a room under the stage, an old pipe organ which hadn't worked for years. It was playing itself!

— One year during the production of a musical, John Kirkpatrick, while rehearsing a solo dance, stopped abruptly and screamed. Others in the cast ran on stage, and they all looked up at the balcony. There, they collectively saw a nebulous "white-clad figure" walk out the door. Rehearsal was suspended as the students combed the building, but again came up empty.

— In the late 1960s, Jeff Rockwell and two of his friends, Scott Black and Paul Hildebrand, both of whom claimed some psychic sensitivities, turned out all of the theater's lights one night after a play rehearsal, and sat in the darkness to see if the ghost lady would appear. They were seated on the edge of the stage in front of the lowered pit. Something flew out of the pit towards them, which they later described as a "rush of air, almost transparent, weird and cold." The mass seemed to chase them as they ran across the stage. it brushed past Hildebrand's ear, and he said it smelled like the "odor of dark crypts."

Although considerable research has been done over the years to determine who Lucinda was, and why she reappears at the hall, nothing definite has ever been determined, although there are several theories. During one seance, students tapped out the name L. Battey, and found she had been active in the theater at the college. She had been killed in either a farming or an auto accident.

Another budding actress, who was to wear a wedding gown in a campus play, died shortly before the play opened. The same dress was later used in another production. One night the leading lady was rehearsing a number when she happened to glance out into the auditorium. She saw the dress "sitting there" as if it were watching her!" Some time later, William and Mary police, on a routine nightly check of the hall, were nearly blinded when a spotlight inexplicably beamed directly into their eyes. They made out a figure in the balcony and raced upstairs. There, they found the same wedding dress folded on a chair. Then a strange noise lured them through the halls of the theater for "quite a long time," but always managed to stay ahead of them.

One wonders, whimsically, what Lucinda might do if MacBeth is ever performed in the hall.

WHO'S THAT IN THE WREN BUILDING?

Retired York County school teacher Edwin Markoff relates an "interesting" experience he had in the historic Wren Building on the William and Mary Campus. The building itself was begun in 1695 and completed four years later. Hugh Jones, author of "The Present State of Virginia," written in 1724, stated that the Wren Building was named for, and indeed designed by the famous British architect, Sir Christopher Wren. The Virginia Landmarks Register, however, says "Wren may or may not have had a hand in the design."

The building was gutted by a fire in 1705, and rebuilt in modified form within the original walls. It burned again in 1859 and in

1862, but the walls survived these fires, too. There also was a major restoration in the late 1920s. Interestingly, the Wren Building is flanked by the President's House and the Brafferton Building, both of which are said to be haunted. (See Volume I.) But until Markoff related his experience at a meeting the author spoke at during September 1995, there had been no reports of any psychic activity at Wren.

Markoff said he was attending a night class in the building in 1967, when a professor's lecture was interrupted by the sound of loud footsteps from the room above. Since no one else was supposed to be in Wren at the time, a search was quickly undertaken and proved unsuccessful. No one appeared to be upstairs.

The professor continued his talk when the footsteps from above were again distinctly heard. Says Markoff: "At that point the professor commented that Sir Christopher Wren must be back to look over his building. Just as soon as he said that, there was a terrible crash from the room above us. It sounded like a chandelier or something like that had smashed to the floor. We were all shaken by it. But when we went back upstairs to look, we found no one and — nothing seemed to be out of place. I don't mind telling you it scared the hell out of everybody there."

Further Revelations at Carter's Grove

(Author's note: In Volume I of "The Ghosts of Williamsburg," I included a chapter titled, "The Puzzling Riddle of the Refusal Room." It was about a particular room at the magnificent Carter's Grove plantation just outside Williamsburg. The legend here was that both George Washington and Thomas Jefferson, at different times, proposed to beautiful ladies, and both were spurned. Two centuries later employees at the mansion, on several occasions, would come in to work and find carnation petals ripped from their vases and strewn across what has become known as the "Refusal Room." There being no rational explanation for this recurring phenomenon, it was speculated that one or the other of the two ladies, now realizing what they had turned down, came back to vent their wrath.

More apparent psychic activity at this site has surfaced since that chapter was first published in 1983. Here then is a sampling:)

THE 'LADY' IN PINK

few years ago an historical interpreter was taking a tour group through Carter's Grove one day when a woman wandered off from the group and headed for the rear door to the house. The interpreter asked her where she was headed. She said she was going outside to talk to the lady in the pink colonial uniform. She had been talking to her and now the lady was outside.

The interpreter said there is no lady in pink, and told the tourist no one was in costume that day. The woman was insistent, however, saying she could see the lady in pink through the window. But when she went outside, the vision had vanished.

THE DISAPPEARING STOWAWAY

Colonial Williamsburg employees have told of frightening experiences related to them by visitors to Carter's Grove. There is a single lane, one-way back road that leads from the historic area several miles to the plantation. It is a rural scenic route that winds through pine and oak forests.

It has been reported that people en route have looked in the back seats of their cars when they were on an isolated stretch of the road and seen a stranger there. Understandably, it unnerved them. Yet, when they reached the open spaces of the Grove acreage, the mysterious stowaway had disappeared. What is particularly unusual about this phenomenon is that a number of tourists, at different times, have told of the same sensation.

THE CARD PLAYING PHANTOMS

Additional research uncovered this, published in the October 1928 issue of a long-extinct magazine of Virginia called "The Black Swan," written by T. Beverly Campbell: "It is said that three pirates are buried beneath its (Carter's Grove) cellar, and we are told that on several occasions these buccaneers have been seen seated in this cellar at a game of cards, but as yet none of those who have seen the apparitions have lingered to watch the game over the shoulders of the pirate ghosts."

THE GHOSTLY LIGHT IN THE JAMES RIVER

There is a rather colorful legend, highly folklorian in nature, and the authenticity of which is sketchy at best, concerning the first English settlement at the Carter's Grove site. Today, it is sometimes told around Halloween by descendants of Indian tribes which once roamed both sides of the James River in this area.

One of the principal reasons for the colony's early survival, from starvation, disease, homesickness, and attacking Indians, was

Carter's Grove

due to the artful diplomacy and negotiating skills of Captain John Smith. He had made peace with the Indians from the time the first white men had landed at Jamestown Island in 1607. Consequently, by providing corn and game, the Indians had greatly helped the settlers make it through what became known as "the starving time."

The Indian chief largely responsible for peaceful relations was the powerful Powhatan. After he died in 1618, he was succeeded by Opechancanough. For four years he built the strength of the regional tribes. Opechancanough had never been at ease with the colonists. He feared they would increase in number to the extent that the Indians would be driven from their homelands entirely.

This fear festered, until it grew into an unabated hatred, and Opechancanough began to plot an all-out attack on the white "enemy." It was easy to whip up strong sentiment among his people, for they were slowly but surely being driven from their favorite hunting and fishing grounds.

The trigger for the attack occurred in March 1622 when two settlers murdered an Indian named Nemattanew. Opechancanough was ready. On the morning of March 22, 1622, members of the Powhatan Confederacy and the Chickahominy tribe entered the colonists's homes and settlements along a seven mile stretch from Jamestown on both sides of the river. The unsuspecting colonists were totally unaware of impending danger, for these Indians worked side by side with them in the fields, and daily traded with them.

The Indians "came to work" without their weapons. But once they had arrived, they grabbed axes, hatchets, knives, hoes, poles and whatever they could find, and began fiercely attacking the colonists — men, women, and children. It was a dreadful slaughter. Within hours, more than 350 settlers had been killed.

One survivor later wrote: "They fell upon the English and basely and barbarously murdered them, not sparing age or sex, man, woman or child. Being at their several works in the house and in the fields, planting corn and tobacco, gardening, making brick, building, sawing and other kinds of husbandry, so sudden was the cruel execution that few or none discerned the weapon or the blow that brought them to destruction."

Plantations at Appomattox, Flower de Hundred, Macock, Westover, Powell's Brook and Martin-Brandon, among others, were destroyed. No life was spared.

The entire colony might well have been wiped out except for a single Indian named Chanco who warned his benevolent "master." A colonist wrote of this incident: "That God had put it into the heart of the converted Indian to reveal the conspiracy by which means Jamestown and many colonists were preserved from their treacheries, was regarded as the most exquisite incident in the life of the colony. For more than 300 of ours died by these pagan infidels, yet thousands of ours were saved by means of one of them alone which was made a Christian. Blessed be God forever Whose mercy endureth forever. Blessed be God Whose mercy is above His justice and far above His works; Who brought this deliverance whereby their souls escaped even as a bird out of the snare of the fowler."

Perhaps nowhere was the massacre as devastating as at Martin's Hundred, a fledgling settlement several miles east of Jamestown, on the James River at a site where the Carter's Grove mansion now stands. Here, 73 settlers were unmercifully killed — and herein is where the legend begins.

It is said that one of the English women at Martin's Hundred was so breathtakingly beautiful that even the Indians were struck with admiration for her. She had long black hair which she tied up with blue and white ribbons. Still, she was not spared in the assault. She was struck down as she stood in the doorway of her cabin. Somehow, bloodied, she managed to crawl to the edge of the woods and tried to hide, but the vengeful Indians caught her again. She was scalped, her precious hair and ribbons torn from her skull. She was left for dead.

Incredibly, the woman again crawled, this time to a trash heap where she remained until the Indians left. She lived till the next day, then died. But her courage, and beauty, has long survived in Indian tradition.

For it is told, till this day, that sometimes, when the fog and mist arise on the river on still nights, the faint moans and screams of the slaughtered colonists at Martin's Hundred can still be heard wafting across the area where a thriving settlement once existed over 375 years ago!

And on clear moonlit evenings a tiny spot of light can be seen dancing in the river. It is, some say, the reflection of the moon on the bare white skull of the beautiful woman who wore blue and white ribbons in her hair and was scalped during the terrible Indian raid of 1622!

CHAPTER 14

The Fearful Force
at Croaker

(Author's note: One of the more interesting letters I have received in recent years was from a young man named John Deusebio, Jr. He said he had enjoyed reading my ghost books, and added, "Although some individuals might consider your work as 'light' reading, I, however, have a great deal of respect for your efforts to preserve pieces of our oral history and cultural heritage for future generations." How could I resist including such a letter?)

John went on to say that he had just read a short piece I did on "The Photographic Spirit of Croaker" (near Williamsburg). "My family has owned a house and property near Croaker since the 1920s, and I lived there during the mid to late 1970s while attending William and Mary. I did not know the people of which you wrote, nor have I ever heard that story before reading it in your book, but I had <u>very similar experiences!</u> Perhaps we have two spirits in that area, or just one that wanders about."

Naturally, as you might imagine, John's letter intrigued me. First, I had to go back to reread about the "Photographic Spirit." It involved some William and Mary students who were renting a 125-year-old farmhouse in Croaker in the mid-1970s, at about the same time that John was there. At first, the two young women and a young man who were living there heard "heavy, booted footsteps and doors slamming in the middle of the night. Then the young man, who slept upstairs, was strangely "afflicted with a series of seizures." Visitors to the house also heard the unexplained noises. One day, a photo was taken of some students sitting on a couch in the house. When the pictures were developed one showed, behind the students, "an ethereal, wispy white mass." One of the coeds had a friend in the Central Intelligence Agency. She gave him the photo and asked him if he would have it examined.

Later, he told her that the "thing" in the picture was a "massive living matter, but not human." He said the agency's past experience with such photos was that ghosts never show up unless "standing directly behind a male human being" (which it was). That mystery was never solved, but after I talked with John Deusebio, following his letter to me, one wonders if John's experiences are not related, somehow, to the photogenic specter. Following is an account, in John's words, of the extraordinary chain of events which happened to him at the same time, in the same location, and perhaps even in the same house!)

"During the summers in those years, I did odd jobs, repair work, to help pay my college expenses. There are a number of seasonal cottages in the area, near or on the York River, and I used to fix them up for the owners, most of whom only came there for the summer season. Well, I had been asked to repair some light switches by the front door. So one day, it was about five or six in the evening, but it was in July so there still was plenty of daylight left, I went over to the house, which was adjacent to where I was staying.

"I entered the house through the back door and proceeded past the hall stairway to the front of the house, where I started to work. I kept getting the overwhelming feeling that someone or something was standing behind me, looking over my left shoulder. I can't really describe it. I kept looking around, and even looked out the front door, but there was no one there. In time, the feeling passed.

"When I finished, I had also been asked to do something on the second floor, so I started up the stairway. I had one foot on the second step and was about to advance to the third step, when a blast — and that's the best way I can define it — a blast of icy cold air hit me. It was like a freezer door opened in your face. It totally enveloped me. I could not move forward. It was like I hit a brick wall. I decided to get the hell out of there as fast as I could.

"I went back to my house and tried to figure what in the world that was. Finally, I decided that it was ridiculous, and that I would go back across the street and try again. This time the frigid blast hit me as I walked out onto my porch. I literally could not move forward. I could move backwards or sideways, but I could not go forward. It was some kind of force. I don't know how else to explain it. Something didn't want me to go over there. So I went back into my house and turned on every light and appliance there.

"Now, let me say here that I don't scare easily. I had done some part-time work in a funeral home in Williamsburg, and I thought I had seen just about everything. I saw murder victims, suicide victims, drowning victims, there wasn't much I hadn't seen, but that force did scare me. I just couldn't understand it.

"Anyway, the next evening I was coming home about 10 at night after having spent some time in Williamsburg. I had an old 1955 Willys Jeep and it was a clear night as I drove down state road 607 to get home. Just as I got abreast of the old farmhouse, the electrical system in the vehicle went crazy. At first, I thought something had shorted out. You can expect that in an old car. But this time it was different. All the arrows on the gauges were dancing back and forth as fast as they could go. The headlights flashed on and off by themselves, and then went out. The ignition went out

'Force House' at Croaker

and the engine died.

"I looked up and froze at what I saw. Right over the hood of the jeep was a wispy, white, cloud-like image. it was about six feet long, two feet wide, and was semi-opaque. It appeared to be just hovering there right in front of me. I thought at first it just must be a patch of low-hanging fog. But then I wondered. I don't remember how long it stayed there, probably just a few seconds, and then it moved off and headed straight towards the old farmhouse where I had met 'the force.'

"As soon as it lifted, the car started right up and everything in the electrical system seemed to be working perfectly. I then drove the couple of hundred yards to my house. Later, I had a real chilling thought as I tried to sort things out. If that cloud or whatever it was had actually been a patch of fog, then it would have moved in the opposite direction from what it did, because the wind off the river was blowing *the other way!*"

CHAPTER 15

The First Spirits in Virginia?

e was — by any measure imaginable — an extraordinary man.

He was, all in one, dynamic, energetic, far-sighted, fearless, and charismatic. He also was acerbic, arrogant, blustery, conceited, and controversial. He often was misunderstood and unjustly maligned.

But he was a remarkable survivor; a man of a thousand lives. He stared down death on dozens of occasions. At times it was as if he had a guardian angel, or a whole band of angels watching over him. He was even accused of having supernatural powers, and, who knows, maybe he did. He was, unquestionably, a legend in his own time and for all time, and, arguably, he did more to save America before it was even known as America, than George Washington, Patrick Henry, and Thomas Jefferson combined.

His name was John Smith.

He was born in Lincolnshire, England, in 1579, and exhibited his famous venturesome spirit from the time he was a boy. In the early 1600s, he ached for adventure, and thus, when the first ill-equipped settlers boarded their ships for the Atlantic crossing to find a new world, John Smith sailed with them. From the start, he was held in disfavor, even arrested before the landing at Jamestown in 1607. But he persevered, and almost immediately set off to explore the area. When the settlers began dying from hunger and disease, it was Smith who helped revive them by bargaining with and bullying regional Indians into providing corn, fresh game

John Smith

and fish. It was Smith who prophetically told his fellow colonists that they should forget their visions of finding gold and other quick riches, and plant crops and build homes out of the Virginia wilderness. More than half of the original settlers died and the colony was almost lost before his advice was finally taken.

Meanwhile, Smith ventured further and further from Jamestown. He followed the mighty James River to its falls in Richmond, seeking a route to the Pacific Ocean. He sailed up the Chickahominy, Pamunkey, and Rappahannock Rivers, among others. Each excursion was fraught with danger. Smith and the other settlers constantly clashed with unfriendly Indians, and he was nearly killed on several occasions. In the most famous of these escapes, he was spared from having his head bashed in by rocks, when Pocahontas rescued him. But he dodged Indian arrows, tomahawks, spears and knives for years, as if some unseen shield protected him.

Once, when he was returning from an exploratory mission to the Chesapeake Bay, he and his men came upon schools of fish so thick they even tried to catch them with frying pans. Smith landed a sinister-looking creature. It turned out to be a sting ray and sank its poisonous tail an inch and a half into the Englishman's wrist. His arm swelled to double its normal size and he became dangerously ill. As he phrased it: "My agony was so great, that I concluded that my death was indeed nigh, and this, my opinion, was shared by the whole company. Foreseeing my death, I directed my grave to be dug on a neighbouring island, a task which was dolefully carried out by my sorrowful companions, and I also ordered my funeral." Again, however, Smith somehow cheated death.

As famine wreaked havoc among the settlers at Jamestown, more and more of them died. It was at this time that Smith reported a possible eerie omen. "Came in company of ravens," he wrote, "which continued amongst them (the settlers) all the time of this mortality and then departed, which for any thing knowne, neither before nor since were ever seene or heard of."

The ominous incident with the ravens, perhaps believed to be harbingers of death, was just one of a number of eerie experiences Smith was to encounter. Many involved the mysterious Indians. One Smith biographer wrote: " . . . During this period he was to witness strange, weird ceremonies which were not comforting to a man in the hands of savage people. Thus with fearful incantations, his body was painted all over, his head covered with the skins of snakes and weasels, some grim fellow would come dancing forth making extraordinary gestures. It was all like some hideous dream, with grotesque cacophonous noises, such as when the mind is delirious and the ear not attuned."

Of one venture into the Potomac River, Smith noted that for the first 30 miles there was no sign of a human being, but they came across a couple of Indians who conducted them up a creek . . . "where the woods had been ambuscaded with several hundred natives all painted, grimed, and disguised, shouting, yelling and crying, as we rather supposed them so many divels."

Smith was told of an apparent supernatural occurrence during another expedition. It was related by a great Indian chief. Smith wrote: "Hee tolde us of a straunge accident lately happened (to) him, and it was (strange). Two deade children, by the extreame passions of their parents, or some dreaming visions, phantasie, or affection (which) moved them againe to revisit their dead carkases: whose benummed bodies reflected to the eyes of the beholders such pleasant delightful countenances, as though they had regained their vital spirits. This, as a miracle, drew many to behold them: all which, (being a great part of his people) not long after died, and not any one escaped!"

Smith reached the mouth of the Potomac River on June 16, 1608, and sailed up it for 30 or more miles. He had heard there was a fabulous gold mine in this vicinity, and friendly Indians led him to the site, but the rumors had proved false; the glittery material in the mine was worthless.

It was during one of Smith's excursions up the Potomac that he came upon an old Indian legend known as the "Curse of the Three Sisters." He penned in his diary of hearing about the "sounds of moaning and sobbing coming from three large rocks jutting out near the Virginia side of the river in the area between where the Chain and Key Bridges now stand.

The legend apparently preceded the first English settlers by as much as a century or more. It has been passed down, tribe to tribe, for half a millennium. In those times, warring Indian factions lived in settlements on both sides of the Potomac, a land that was rich in food, fish, game and natural resources. Among the most feared leaders were the tribal medicine men, who were believed to have magical powers.

The story Smith heard, as told in recent years by John Alexander in his fine book on Washington-area ghosts, and in various other newspaper and magazine articles, centered around three beautiful daughters of one of these medicine men.

They were in love with three young braves. One day the braves ventured across the Potomac to fish near the northern shore; food was desperately short in their village, due to the near-continuous fighting which had been waged between tribes for months. The braves, however, were overtaken by members of an enemy faction, taken prisoner, tortured and scalped.

All of this was done in full view of the braves' villagers across the river. Among the horrified witnesses were the three young maidens. They almost immediately hatched a plot to seek revenge. They would, they said, cross the river and give themselves to the murderers of their loved ones. They then would subject them to the evil magic of their father, insuring slow, torturous deaths for the ones who killed their lovers.

It was with this in mind that they set out one day to cross the Potomac in a makeshift raft. They never reached the other side. A swift current swept them downriver towards the Chesapeake Bay. It was said that the three women, realizing their fate, clasped their arms around each other and "shouted a curse." If they could not successfully cross the Potomac at that point, then no one else would be able to cross there either, ever! They then jumped into the surging waters and drowned!

It was passed along that as this tragedy unfolded, the sky darkened, thunder rumbled overhead, and lightning bolts seared the shorelines near where the maidens had disappeared; near the Three Sisters rocks. According to author Alexander and others, "to this day," disaster has befallen anyone who has attempted to cross the river at the site. Harbor police say there are several drownings here each year involving swimmers, fishermen and boaters. Further, in the 1970s, another huge storm caused flood waters which swept away construction framework at the proposed site for a new bridge near the Three Sisters rocks. Many ascribed this to the long-remembered curse.

In fact, old time rivermen contend that when a mournful cry is heard during a storm, it is an omen that there will soon be another drowning. The spell cast 500 years ago, seemingly still holds. It was the same curse John Smith heard about in the early 1600s, and might represent the first known occurrence of ghostly phenomena in Virginia.

* * * * * *

DODGING THE ANGEL OF DEATH

Did Captain John Smith have some sort of magical psychic shield protecting him during his precarious early days in Virginia; some inexplicable phenomena which saved his life a number of times when it appeared certain he was about to die at the hands of hostile Indians and others?

At least an allusion to this was recorded by Professor Virgil A. Lewis in his 1897 book, "Virginia and Virginians." He wrote of the time Smith, while venturing up the Chickahominy River, was captured by area Indians. Here is what he said:

"His (Smith's) captors carried him before their chief, who received him with all the pomp and ceremony known at a savage court. A long consultation was held to determine the fate of the distinguished prisoner, and it seemed that the <u>death angel</u> which had hovered around him all along his journey of life was about to claim the victory. The consultation terminated unfavorably; the executioners rushed forward and dragged their prisoner to a large stone upon which it had been decided his head should be crushed.

"The awful moment was come; the club was raised that was to dash out his brains, and thus end his toils and difficulties, and with them the hope of Virginia. But an advocate appeared as unexpectedly as would have been an *angel just descended from heaven*, to ask his release. It was none other than Pocahontas, the chieftain's own favorite daughter, who stepped forth and begged that the prisoner might be spared, and when she found her entreaties unavailing, she seized his head and placed it beneath her own to protect it from the fatal blow. Powhatan could not resist the pleadings of his favorite child, and yielded to her wishes.

"Smith was released and allowed to live."

CHAPTER 16

Caught in a Colonial Time Warp

t was on historic Jamestown Island, a spit of heavily-wooded land jutting into the mighty James River, that America's first band of settlers chose to begin a new life. It was here that they anchored and came ashore for good in May 1607. And, it was here, 364 years later, that a small group of the early adventurers apparently "returned" for a brief period in an extraordinary occurrence witnessed by Gerry McDowell of Virginia Beach and her late husband, Gus.

Both Gerry and Gus liked to travel, and often visited regional sites in the off season. It was on such an excursion to Jamestown Island in 1971 that the "event" happened. They were there very early on a chilly autumn morning, because, as Gerry says, "we liked to be out when no one was around so we could enjoy the solitude, and Gus liked to feed the animals."

The story is best told in Gerry's own words, as follows: "I can remember it as clearly as if it happened yesterday, although it now has been more than 25 years. It was real early on a Sunday morning, about 6 a.m. It was damp and misty. You could see the fog coming off the river. I was listening to one of those audio recordings which told all about the first settlement, when I had the strangest sensation. There was a deathly stillness in the air.

"I turned around and there, coming down a path toward us was a group of about 20 people, men, women and children. They were all dressed in colonial costume. The men wore knickers with either black or white stockings and shoes with buckles. They had

Jamestown Church

on jacket blouses with wide white collars and very broad brimmed hats. The ladies were wearing long gray or black dresses, with shawls over their shoulders, and bonnets.

"They were very animated. The men and women were talking and laughing, and waving their arms as they walked. The children were running in and out of the group. I thought at first that it might be a troop of actors who were coming to participate in a play or something. I looked at Gus, and he saw them, too. We stood together and watched as they approached us.

"It was then that we realized there was something different. While they seemed to be talking, there was no sound whatsoever. Instead there was only an icy silence. They didn't appear to be ghosts, because I think most ghosts are wispy or transparent, and they weren't. You couldn't see through them. And then we noticed. They <u>were</u> ghosts, because they were not walking on the ground! They were elevated above it by a few inches.

"Gus and I froze. We stood still and didn't say a thing. We felt together that any movement or sound on our part would dissolve them. On they came. They marched right by us without noticing us. It was as if we weren't there. We could have reached out and touched them, but we didn't. They moved past us and walked straight up the path to the church. When we turned to follow them, we could barely believe our eyes. The church had transformed from its present state to how it must have looked in the early 1600s, complete with steeple and all! Gus and I both gasped.

"They opened the door and, one by one, went inside. When the last gentleman entered, he turned and appeared to stare at us. Gus said he had a smile on his face. I didn't see that, but he slammed the door forcefully. Again, there was no sound. We stood there for a few seconds in silence, transfixed. And then the church appeared in its present state again.

"Neither one of us was afraid of ghosts, so we were not really scared. Still, it was minutes before either of us could speak. Then Gus finally said, 'nobody is going to believe this!' We went into the church. It was empty! I don't know much about such things, but I think now that we had somehow gotten into a time warp for that brief instant. I have heard about such things, although I don't really understand them. But how else can you explain what happened! All I know is that it was a once in a lifetime experience that I will never forget."

Is Jamestown Island Forever Cursed?

reasonable case could be made that Jamestown Island, the site of the first permanent English settlement in America, could be cursed. Certainly, there has been more than enough tragedy and misfortune over the past nearly 400 years to warrant such a foreboding claim. Two-thirds of the first 105 Englishmen who landed here on May 14, 1607, were dead within eight months, and of the first 500 settlers who made the long and arduous crossing of the Atlantic Ocean to reach Jamestown, only 60 survived.

Despite Captain John Smith's initial observation that the island was "a verie fit place for the erecting of a great cittie," it was, instead, a horrible location. Consider some 17th century accounts:

— Mrs. Ann Cotton: ". . . It is low ground, full of marshes and swamps, which make the aire especially in the summer insalubritious and unhealthy. It is not at all replenished with springs of fresh water, and that which they have in their wells, brackish, ill scented, penurious and not grateful to the stomack."

— George Percy: "Our men were destroyed with cruell diseases, as Swellings, Flixes, Burning fevers, and by Warres (with Indians), and some departed suddenly, but for the most part they died of meere famine. There were never Englishmen left in a forreine Countrey in such miserie as wee were in this new discovered Virginia."

— David Pietersen de Vries: "They say that during the months of June, July, and August, it is very unhealthy; that their people who have lately arrived from England, die during these months, like cats and dogs . . . "

The disastrous toll in human life was further advanced by the fact that most of the first settlers were ill equipped for such a harsh environment. Many were "refined gentlemen," who had few skills or the inclination to cope with the forging of a colony in the wilderness. This alone caused much strife and hardship. As John Rolfe, the husband of Pocahontas, wrote in 1620: "I speake on my owne experience for these 11 yeres, I never amongst so few, have seene so many falsehearted, envious and malicious people . . ." And Governor Dale said, in 1611: "Everie man allmost laments himself of being here, and murmers at his present state."

In January 1608, a terrible fire ravaged Jamestown, and, two years later most of the survivors died during a period known as "the starving time." Starvation drove some to cannibalism and others to madness. So many died so fast that they were hastily buried, without benefit of coffins, in mass shallow graves, in an effort to hide the vulnerability of the precarious colony from Indians.

In 1622, an Indian massacre killed more colonists, but even this was less threatening than rampant disease which claimed a greater number of victims. Historian Lyon Gardiner Tyler wrote: "Jamestown was literally the grave of the first settlers. The fatality among them, produced by famine and diseases of the climate, was almost unprecedented." To this, Carl Bridenbaugh, author of "Jamestown, 1544-1699," added: "The story of Jamestown is one of continous tragedy — wars, disease, death, fires . . . " Indeed, it is a wonder that any early Jamestowners made it.

The town burned to the ground again in 1676, when rebellious Nathaniel Bacon and his men torched it. It was rebuilt, only to once more succumb to flames on Halloween, 1698. As Lyon Tyler put it: "The evil genius of misfortune still pursued the unfortunate metropolis."

It was only then, as the 18th century approached, that the colony leaders, perhaps believing that there was indeed a curse on their site, decided to move the capital inland to what was then known as Middle Plantation — Williamsburg. Most of Jamestown Island then lapsed into a tomb-like silence that has lasted for 300 years. In 1716, John Fontaine wrote: "The town (Jamestown) consists of a church, a court house and three or four brick houses . . . but all is gone to ruin."

Sometime early in the 18th century, probably in the 1720s, a family named Ambler acquired a sizeable tract of land here and built a formidable home. Despite the isolation, the Amblers were prominent citizens. Richard Ambler, for example, ran the ferry from Jamestown Island across the James River to Surry in the 1740s, and another Ambler, in 1766, was an esteemed member of the Virginia House of Burgesses.

In an article in the Southern Literary Messenger, published in 1837, the writer notes: "The greater part of the island was in possession of the Ambler family for several generations . . . The soil is well adapted to the growth of corn, wheat, oats and palma christi. The island and surrounding country abound in game of almost every description — partridges, pheasants, wild turkeys, waterfowl and deer."

The writer went on to say: "Here are the tombs of several other persons eminent for talent and usefulness during the early age of the colony. They are, however, in a very ruinous and mutilated state . . . In digging the foundation of a house in the island some time since, the workmen discovered several human skeletons. Indeed, these may be found in many places near the site of the town. Jamestown was literally the grave of the first settlers. The fatality among them, produced by famine and diseases of the climate was almost unprecedented."

The mansion itself was Georgian, with a dominant central structure flanked by dependencies "to give the whole edifice line, proportion and balance." One author reported that "a surviving photograph of the plantation house . . . showed it to be a bleak and grim pile devoid of any environmental embellishment save for a dirt path flanked by rows of paper mulberries, trees renowned for their gnarled and forbidding appearance."

There is, too, a sad legend associated with the Ambler home, that is reminiscent of an earlier "love tragedy" nearby at the James River plantation — Westover. Here, in 1737, Evelyn Byrd, the daughter of William Byrd, II, pined away and is said to have died of a broken heart because her father would not let her marry the man she loved. Evelyn is said to occasionally reappear, in ghostly form, at Westover.

On Jamestown Island, a young lady named Lydia Ambler allegedly fell in love with a soldier named Alexander Maupin during the time of the American Revolutionary War. They were hastily married in August 1776, and he left, soon after, to fight for American independence. He never returned. It is not known if he was killed in battle, or just abandoned his unhappy bride. Tradition says she waited anxiously for him, often spending the

The Ambler Ruins

day on the banks of the James River, peering ever hopefully for him to return. Finally, in despair, she took her own life.

The curse continued when, in 1781, American hero-turned-traitor, Benedict Arnold sailed up the James and destroyed a number of plantation houses, including the Ambler mansion. It was rebuilt, only to be burned again during the Civil War. Once more, it was reconstructed. Then, in the 1890s, flames razed it again, leaving only ruins which still stand as silent sentinels to the cruel fates.

And, in recent years, there have been "incidents" recorded that the pale and desolate wraith of Lydia Ambler returns to the site, still searching for her lost lover. National park employees have told of seeing the apparition of a woman, wearing a gown of the 18th century, roaming the grounds. They know this is not a reenactor dressed in period costume, because the woman vanishes before their eyes!

One person who has had frightful experiences here is Traci Poole of Hampton, Virginia. Traci is a psychic. She sees and senses things others do not. She is, in paranormal terms, gifted . . . or cursed with such abilities.

For example, in 1991, when Traci's step-mother died of cancer, her vision appeared to Traci, who was miles away at the time. At the moment of death, the step-mother was visible to Traci, her arms outstretched, smiling, and surrounded by a purplish-colored aura. She had previously made a pact with Traci, telling her if she could come back from the beyond to communicate, she would.

Three years later, when Traci was pregnant with her daughter, Amber, Traci began hemorrhaging. Doctors told her that either she or her daughter would not make it alive through the birth. Traci told them to save the baby. As they were preparing Traci for a C-section, her step-mother's apparitional figure appeared to her, again smiling and with her arms outstretched. Traci thought her step-mother had come "to get her." The next conscious thing she remembered was someone touching her and saying, "Traci, you have a beautiful baby girl." "It was a miracle both of us were alive," Traci says today.

Traci, for some inexplicable reason, is drawn to Jamestown Island and the Ambler mansion. "I can't tell you why, but I am obsessed with the place," she says. "I've had some very strong sensations there. There have been times when I've been on the island and I had to get out of there. I could hardly breathe. At the foot of the large cross memorial there, I have heard children and women talking, and I don't mean tourists. These voices were from another time. I have seen Indian images there of barebreasted women, with bits of shell and bone necklaces. It freaked me out."

Traci also is deeply moved each time she visits the Ambler ruins. "I get the profound impression that the house never should have been built, that it was doomed from the start. Sometimes I can see people dancing there, but there also is a very dark side. There is a feeling of a presence against the liveability of the house. I know there was much sadness and tragedy here. I get goosebumps just thinking about it."

Amid the mass graves of America's first settlers, and the ghosts of past residents, the curse — or as Lyon Tyler put it, "The evil genius of misfortune" — apparently lives on at Jamestown Island.

CHAPTER 18

The Charismatic Cavalier & the Vengeful Governor

he contrasts between the two men couldn't have been greater. One was 70-years-old and was the long-time governor of the Colony of Virginia. He was growing deaf, had a mercurial temper, harbored grudges, and ruled with a tyrannical hand. Some suspected he was approaching the early stages of senility. Once loved and respected, he was now feared and hated.

The other was young, 28, high-spirited, charismatic, intellectual, a masterful orator and a natural leader. Though he had been in Virginia for only a short time, he had already established himself as a fearless, dynamic personality.

The two men were on a collision course which would make an indelible mark on colonial history. In fact, some experts believe their clash was the chief precursor to the American Revolution which would take place a century later.

The year was 1676. The older man was William Berkeley, governor of Virginia. The younger man was Nathaniel Bacon, Jr., a landowner and farmer.

Berkeley had first come to the colony as governor in 1642, and then had been well received. He was a talented young man with a magnetic personality. He encouraged crop diversification, exhibited "statesmanship of a high order," and was considered a fair and able ruler. But he had stayed in power too long. As he grew older, his popularity waned. He had not held any elections for 14 years, causing widespread dissent.

But perhaps the biggest complaint against the governor, in 1676, was that he seemed to have lost his incentive for protecting the colonists against marauding Indian attacks. Earlier, especially after the great Indian massacre of white settlers in 1644, Berkeley personally led the charge against the attackers. But now, even though nearly 500 colonists had been killed in the early months of 1676, he refused to commission his followers to seek vengeance.

It was this refusal, principally, that forced the young Bacon into a leadership role. Incensed, after his own overseer had been murdered, Bacon, backed by alarmed citizens in what is now Charles City and Henrico counties, took charge. Without approval from the governor, he led an expedition against the Occaneechees, slaughtered 100 of them, and burned their village to the ground. When Berkeley heard of this, he charged Bacon with "treason and rebellion," captured him and brought him to Jamestown. Here, the governor exclaimed: "Now I behold the greatest rebel that ever was in Virginia." But realizing that Bacon had become a popular hero to the people, Berkeley relented and pardoned him.

Bacon did not trust Berkeley, however, and with a force of more than 100 armed men returned to Jamestown in June, where he confronted the governor with his request for a commission to go after the attacking Indians. Berkeley was infuriated, but when Bacon ordered his men to aim their cocked guns at the windows of the statehouse, the governor had little choice but to grant the commission.

But no sooner had Bacon and his men begun chasing the Indians, when Berkeley renounced the commission, called Bacon a traitor, and said he would raise an army to go after him. But two things happened which caused the governor to retreat instead. First, Bacon, using fiery oratory, raised a force of 1,300 men, and second, Berkeley's own militia men were "completely unwilling" to go after Bacon. Consequently, the governor abandoned both Jamestown and his own palatial home at Green Spring, and fled across the Chesapeake Bay to the Eastern Shore.

Bacon then went in pursuit of the Pamunkey Indians in the Dragon Swamp, and while he was occupied here, Berkeley and his adjutants managed to retake Jamestown. Bacon reassembled his troops and stormed the colonial capital. The governor's soldiers virtually threw down their arms and ran. They had little heart to fight a man many of them believed was right in his cause. Berkeley again sailed to the Eastern Shore. Bacon then had Jamestown burned.

It was then, in the fall of 1676, that fate intervened and ended what has become known as "Bacon's Rebellion." The months of hard fighting and marching through swamps and thick woods finally took its toll on the young leader. As historian Virginius Dabney phrased it: "He (Bacon) had been under constant strain since the arduous expedition in the spring which took him hundreds of miles through the wilderness against the Occaneechees. Then came the marches and countermarches against Berkeley's forces, as well as the Pamunkeys, across trackless terrain and in abominable weather combining stifling heat with almost uninterrupted rain and enervating humidity. All this lowered his resistance. In the soggy trenches before Jamestown

Governor Berkeley
(Rendering courtesy of the Colonial
Williamburg Foundation.)

Map of Virginia
at time of
Bacon's Rebellion

he is believed to have contracted the dysentery which carried him off a few weeks later."

He died on October 26, 1676, at the home of Major Thomas Pate on Portopotank Creek in Gloucester County, not far from the town of West Point. What happened next has remained an unsolved mystery for more than 300 years. As Dabney wrote: "Bacon was buried secretly, lest perchance Governor Berkeley seek to inflict indignities upon his corpse." But where?

Author Mary Newton Stanard, in her book, "The Story of Bacon's Rebellion," published in 1907, says: "Those who had loved the Rebel in life were faithful to him in death, and tenderly laid his body away beyond the reach of the insults of his enemies. So closely guarded was the secret of the place and manner of his burial that it is unto this day a mystery; but tradition has it that stones were placed in his coffin and he was put to bed beneath the deep waters of the majestic York River."

But Philip Alexander Bruce, author of "The Virginia Plutarch," published in 1929, wrote: "His corpse was committed at night to the waters of one of the inlets, and to this day the exact spot where his bones repose is unknown." Over the years there have been several attempts to find Bacon's body, believed by many to be submerged in shallow creek or inlet waters in Gloucester County, but all the searches have been in vain.

With their leader dead, Bacon's followers could not keep up the cause, and the rebellion collapsed. A number of Bacon's key lieutenants were hunted down and captured. It was then that Governor Berkeley openly demonstrated his cruel vengeance. Despite a plea from King Charles II of England for leniency, Berkeley had 23 of Bacon's men executed, after "trials devoid of dignity and fairness." Most were hanged. He also confiscated their estates and harshly treated their wives and children. Such vindictiveness contributed to the termination of Berkeley's reign in Virginia. He was called back to England and died a short time later.

As one York County resident summed up the tragic ending for Bacon's men, "the Hangman (was) more dreadful to the Baconians, then their General was to the Indians; as it is counted more honourable, and less terable, to dye like a Souldier, then to be hang'd like a dogg."

Considering all the traumatic deaths involved, the unresolved mission of Nathaniel Bacon, and the undying vengefulness of Governor Berkeley, it might be assumed that such would be just cause for the return, in spirit form, of one or more of the participants. Perhaps.

There are, for example, a number of psychic manifestations which have taken place at Bacon's Castle in Surry County — a 17th century mansion in which Bacon's followers hid out during the rebellion. These have included unaccountable footsteps, "horrible moaning" in the attic when no one is there, objects being flung across rooms by unseen hands, and, most frightening, the occasional appearance of a "pulsating, red ball of fire" which soars 30 to 40 feet in the air over castle grounds and then disappears. Some attribute these incidents to the ghosts of Bacon's men who were unmercifully hanged.

There are additional clues at the site of Green Spring, Governor Berkeley's mansion near Williamsburg. Although the house is no longer standing, a spirit or two there may still be sensed. Writing in the Colonial Williamsburg Magazine in 1996, historian, archeologist and author Ivor Noel Hume had this to say: "Those who believe in the supernatural will tell you that places once the scene of great emotional or physical stress retain their energy and can release it years, even centuries, later to those of us tuned to the right wave length.

"I visited the Green Spring site at dusk on January 22, 1996 — 319 years to the day since a victorious Governor Berkeley returned to oust its defenders and begin the reign of terror that so horrified the colony.

"The trees were still; the ground was hard, cold, and crackled under foot. The headlights of my parked car barely carried to the only still standing ruin — the one known as the jail and believed to have housed Berkeley's doomed prisoners. I listened there for the rattle of fetters, of the pleading voices of the weak, the cold, and the hungry. . . . I heard a snapping twig as the fall of a gavel ending the court martial that sent Captain Crewes stumbling past me down the dirt road to his death at Glasshouse Point.

"Suddenly a chill wind blew across the open field rustling the dead grass; I pulled my coat tighter around me and was anxious to be gone. At Green Spring there should be, must be, ghosts."

And finally, there is this, written by a newspaper reporter more than 40 years ago in a Halloween article about the spirits of Colonial Williamsburg . . . "There's Royal Governor Berkeley . . . last seen some 270-odd years ago when his palace (Green Spring) burned . . . not a trace of him until the restoration started here 27 years ago. Now, he's supposed to sit slouched in an armchair at the restored palace smoking his pipe and (disdainfully) dropping an ash or two on the royal rug."

CHAPTER 19

A Host of Haunting Humor

o ghosts have a sense of humor? Possibly. Sometimes spookiness can be downright humorous. Consider the following examples:

FIVE FIGURES RISING FROM THE MIST

few years ago, in the midst of a severe winter, tourism was way down in Williamsburg. So one day when five colonial historical interpreters were invited to visit an old church in neighboring New Kent County and learn of its history, they readily accepted. They were driven to the site, and because of the cold weather, they were wearing long hooded cloaks over their colonial costumes.

After their tour they came outside and sat down on a bench in front of the cemetery adjacent to the church to wait for their ride back to town. It was now nearing dark and it was drizzling slightly.

Pretty soon they heard a vehicle coming up the country road. Assuming it was their ride, these five women in their colonial costumes with long cloaks and hoods . . .in the dusk . . . in the mist . . . arose in unison with the shadowy tombstones in the background . . .

And it wasn't their ride. It was a tourist from New Jersey. The ladies said he took one look at them . . . and promptly drove into a tree!

And never got out of his car to examine the damage.

Aunt Pratt

AUNT PRATT STRIKES AGAIN

In the first "Ghosts of Williamsburg," the colorful legend of Aunt Pratt, or rather her portrait, was told. Aunt Pratt was actually Martha Hill Griffard, who died in 1752. Being a member of the Hill family, her portrait hangs at beautiful Shirley Plantation on historic Route 5 about halfway between Williamsburg and Richmond. The Hills and Carters have owned Shirley for something like 10 or 12 generations.

Some years ago, when a new generation of the family moved into the mansion, someone apparently didn't care for the portrait, and relegated it to the attic. Noises of furniture being moved around in the attic, and the sounds of a woman crying were heard, but nothing was ever found. Finally it was decided that maybe Aunt Pratt was unhappy up there, so her portrait was brought back downstairs, and the mysterious phenomena ceased.

Sometime later, however, when the portrait was loaned to the Virginia travel office for an exhibit in New York, the manifestations reoccurred. Workmen came in one day to find Aunt Pratt off the wall, on the floor, and, in their words, halfway to the exit. And when they locked her in a closet at night for security, the sobbing of a woman was clearly heard through the door. Once the portrait was returned to Shirley and hung in its proper place, Aunt Pratt was not heard from again — with one exception — giving rise to speculation that her spirit may still be active.

One day in 1998, a male tourist was standing beneath the portrait as Aunt Pratt's story was being related by a tour guide.

He turned his back and scoffed out loud, calling the legend a lot of baloney.

According to the guide and other witnesses, just as he said this, the doors of a large armoire beneath the portrait suddenly sprang open and struck the man smartly on his backside!

The room emptied in 10 seconds.

ESCAPE ATTEMPT FROM AN OPEN GRAVE

 hings got pretty scary for a while in the late 1800s around old St. Luke's Church just east of Smithfield and across the James River southeast of Williamsburg. In fact, it got so bad townspeople would go out of their way not to go near the place.

Described as an "ancient and beautiful Gothic edifice," St. Luke's was built in 1632, and is the oldest brick Protestant church in America. Traditionally called "Old Brick Church," it originally was in Warrosquyoake Parish, which was divided several times between 1642 and 1752, when it became Newport Parish.

According to local legend, inhabitants of the area buried county records and the vestry books in an old trunk during the Revolutionary War when they heard of an intended raid by British troops. Unfortunately, after the war when the trunk was dug up, many of the records crumbled to pieces.

The church was not used and remained in neglect from 1830 until the 1890s when it was restored. There is reason enough to suspect a haunting story or two involving St. Luke's. Buried in the adjoining graveyard, for example, are the remains of many civil War soldiers, and there have been a few residents who claim they have heard moans and cries emanating from the plots late at night.

In the days prior to restoration, the church was in sad disrepair. Most of the roof was gone. Nevertheless, it still offered a semblance of shelter on the storm-tossed night long ago when a rider on horseback approached it. No sooner had he tied his horse, and

St. Luke's

propped himself up against a wall in a dry corner, when something in the graveyard caught his eye.

He described it as a "white, fluttering" sensation. Whatever it was, blurred by the rain and hazy in the darkness, it appeared to be trying to escape an open grave site.

Whatever it was, the lone rider had seen enough. He and his steed galloped away toward town at breakneck speed. When word spread of the "unsettled spirit," Smithfield residents absolutely refused to go near the site.

However, the mystery was soon solved. One fearless person walked across the cemetery in broad daylight to investigate. What did he find?

A rather large goose had fallen into the open grave and couldn't quite manage an escape on its own, thus explaining the frantic white fluttering.

NEVER MAKE FUN OF A GHOST

hen Payne Tyler, mistress of Sherwood Forest in Charles City County west of Williamsburg, had "enough" of the ghostly presence of the "gray lady," (see separate chapter) , she sat down and had a talk with the spirit. Payne says the manifestations quieted considerably after that.

Some time later her cousin came over for a visit and the two ladies sat down in the library. When Payne related how she had had a chat with the apparition, her cousin laughed heartily and chided Payne. "That's crazy," she said. "Who ever heard of talking with a ghost?"

Just as she said this, a powerful blast of frigid air rushed down the chimney of the fireplace and swept through the room, thoroughly chilling Payne and her guest. And then the shutters on the window started banging sharply back and forth, although there was no wind whatsoever.

The frightened cousin, got up and abruptly left — and didn't return to the house for several years!

THE CURIOUS FUNERAL OF BILLY GILLIAM

 long-standing legend in Williamsburg is based on the unusual funeral of a man named Billy Gilliam, sometime after the Civil War.

It should be noted that there apparently are several versions of this particular incident, and also that it probably has been considerably embellished over the years. While it is not ghost-related, it is a rather colorful tale in itself.

Billy was a young man when he died of unspecified causes. Like many others in town, he had been a member of the "Wise Light Infantry," a group of military volunteers who had organized under the leadership of a Dr. Wise, then a professor at the College of William and Mary. So it was decided to give Billy a military funeral.

When members of his unit arrived at his house, they found Billy laid out in his casket in his full Wise Light Infantry uniform. This seemed to cause a problem, since the group had not paid for the uniforms yet. A quick decision was held and it was decided to strip the body of the coat, which could be used by another member.

What happened next seems to be shrouded in mystery. The detail of young men started up the street with the coffin as their little band played "Hop Light, Ladies, the Cake's All Dough."

It wasn't exactly a tune designed for the occasion, but the band only knew two numbers "Hop Light" and "Dixie."

Up Duke of Gloucester Street they went, headed for the cemetery, when all of a sudden a young boy rushed up to the procession and stopped it. He was out of breath and stammering, and there was some confusion.

Finally, he got his message out. Somehow, back at Billy's house when his coat was taken off, his body was never placed back in the coffin. It was left at home!

So the Wise Light Infantry turned around, marched back to the house, placed Billy in the coffin, and headed back up the street, still marching to "Hop Light, Ladies."

After the service at the cemetery, Captain Wise ordered a volley to be fired over the grave. But there was another slip up. The men mistakenly had been issued live cartridges instead of the usual blanks. One of the stray shots killed a cow in a nearby pasture who had wandered too close to the scene.

The unit was compelled to pay for the cow, which depleted the infantry's treasury and led to its financial ruin and subsequent disbandment.

PAINTING AN APPARITION BLACK

On August 6, 1767, the Virginia Gazette, printed in Williamsburg, published the following letter describing a most bizarre encounter with the supernatural.

Seems a gentleman of means, newly married, was awakened late one stormy night by his bride, who said she thought there was a ghost in the room. He "was so terrified that he immediately jumped out of bed, and knowing there was a bottle of holy water in a closet in his room, he walked to take it out, without any more light than that of the constant lightening, and soon began to sprinkle his Lady, himself and even the very furniture to engage, without doubt, the protection of Providence.

". . . He returned to bed pretty well composed, and began to value himself highly on the efficacy of his operation; but how great was his surprise when, at daylight, he awoke and turned toward his Lady, who he found as black as a curlpated inhabitant of Africa, and all the bedding, tapestry and furniture of the room of the same melancholy complexion."

What had happened? In the darkness the night before, as he reached for the holy water, he instead snatched up a bottle of ink!

SAY THAT AGAIN

n the Bruton Parish cemetery visitors may do a double take when they come to the following grave-stone:
"To the Memory of Mr. Charles Hunt late of this parish.
He died the 11th day of Oct 1794 Aged 41 years.
Regretted by all who knew him."

IT MUST BE HELL

(Author's note: I get a lot of letters from ghost lovers all over the country. One I cherish was from a lady in Philadelphia who said that she and her husband met in Williamsburg. Then she added: "We have been marred for 26 and a half years.")

CHAPTER 20

More Historic Hauntings at the Moore House

(Author's note: In Volume I, I wrote that "History comes alive in more ways than one at the Moore House set amidst the Yorktown battlefield. It was in this wooden frame structure that on the afternoon of October 18, 1781, representatives of General George Washington and Lord Cornwallis met to negotiate terms of the British surrender to the American forces, in effect ending the Revolutionary War." The house is believed to have been built in the early 1700s.

The paranormal activity here is thought to be created by Augustine Moore, Jr., an early resident, who allegedly was killed by a bullet in the crossfire of the battlefield during the siege of Yorktown. Either Moore, or someone, occasionally returns to the house to "take a nap" in the upstairs bedroom. National Park employees have reported that they have many times found a "deep impression" on the bed covers after maintenance people had made the bed and no one else had been in the house. "Something" also sits in a red velvet chair in the downstairs room where the peace negotiations took place. Psychic experts have said they sensed a "strong presence" in the bedroom, and one saw the vision of "a man dressed in colonial-era clothes looking out the bedroom window.

Then, in 1995, I got a letter and tape recording from a young lady then living in Yorktown named Kim Schultz. This is what she had to say:)

"I have always been interested in historical places and tried to visit every place I knew of in the Tidewater (Virginia) area.

"My favorite 'haunt' (excuse the pun) now is Yorktown. I went there and still go there when I'm feeling down or need to be alone with myself and just think. My wanderings occasionally took me to Moore House, which was never opened to the public on the days I chose to be there. Consequently, I usually had the house and grounds to myself.

"At first, I never ventured too close to it. As I eventually got bolder, I would stand outside the yard gate and peruse the front of the house. For some unexplainable reason, I felt uncomfortable about looking up at the bedroom windows. I felt a kind of sadness coming from the windows.

"The next time I saw the house I was walking from the cliff straight to the yard gate, meditating upon one thing or another. Subconsciously, I intended just to walk right up the little path to the front of the house, but my legs just stopped at the gate. I came out of my daydream and realized that I couldn't walk past the gate. Not that anything physical was barring me, but, instinctively, I knew that someone *did live there,* and I felt like I was trespassing.

"Several months later," she continues, "my mother and I were visiting Yorktown on a Sunday. I had hoped Moore House would be open so I brought a tape recorder, because of something I had seen on television of people recording ghosts on tape. Well, Moore House was open and a tour guide was there to show us around.

"I had my tape recorder going the whole time, and even stayed behind upstairs after everyone else had left the building so that I could tape in each of the bedrooms. By the way, I did notice on that day an indentation in one of the white-blanketed beds, as if someone had been lying in it."

Kim and her mother went home after the tour and Kim listened to the tape. "For about 10 minutes or so into the tape, it was pretty much just the tour guide talking," she says. "Then he finished his speech and allowed us to roam around the house as he answered random questions from people. Even before he had finished his speech, I had moved inside the first room on the left, which seemed to be a sitting room. I had my tape recorder extended away from my body toward the room. For the first 30 seconds or so, I had been the only person in the room.

"As I was listening to the tape, my eyes suddenly popped open.

Moore House

I played it back. It sounded like a voice being played in slow motion, like the old record players when you left the needle on the record and turned the machine off. The voice kind of wound down. I played it a dozen times. The tape I had used was a fresh one, never been recorded on. The noise in the background was the same, it hadn't altered like the strange sound did. I went immediately and played it for my mother and she got spooked, too.

"I must have played it 20 times over and she said she could not think what could have made a sound like that. I then took the tape to work with me and played it for four different people. None of them could think what could have caused the sound. They also said they felt creepy listening to it. . . I also heard on the tape a double knocking noise when I was alone upstairs taping the bedrooms."

(Author's note: Kim Schultz sent a copy of the tape to me and asked if I could find a rational explanation for it. I played the tape. The sounds she described are there. I have no rational explanation!)

CHAPTER 21

Active Spirits at the Cole Digges House

(Author's note: In October 1998, I received a letter in a thick envelope from Carter R. Allen of Waynesboro, an attorney. I am always leery when I receive mail from lawyers. You never know, some descendent of a ghost I had written about might have taken offense and wanted to sue me. However, in this instance, I was pleasantly surprised. Here is what Mr. Allen had to say: "My wife's aunt and her husband lived in the Cole Digges House in Yorktown the last years of their lives and experienced a ghost, which my daughter, Mary Dudley Allen Eggleston (also a member of the Virginia Bar), wrote about in her high school days. I thought you might find it interesting so I am taking the liberty of enclosing it."

I did find it interesting. Here not only was an historic house, allegedly haunted, of which I had not heard of or written about previously — but there were also some unusual phenomena.

Cole Digges was a direct descendant of governor Edward Digges — and he was the son of Dudley Digges and Susannah Cole Digges, she being the daughter of Colonel William Cole of Warwick County. The house Cole inherited was built in 1705 at the corner of Main and Read Streets in Yorktown. The Digges family remained here until 1784, three years after the American Revolutionary War ended.)

ary Dudley Allen Eggleston wrote her paper on the house in August 1977. She said it was

Cole Digges House

an "Early American styled home, accompanied with high, pine paneled ceilings, large beautiful old oaken doors, and magnificent interior woodwork." She added that after the Digges family left, the house, at various times, served as a general store, a bank, a restaurant, and a hotel.

"My great aunt, Mary Louise Williamson, lives (1977) in Yorktown. Her husband, Charlie A. Williamson, died this past March. Before Charlie died, he and Mary Louise told me in great detail the events leading up to an acute description of the ghost they have been housing. Being such an old home and having so many different kinds of people building the character of the Cole Digges House, (here Mary Eggleston quotes her late uncle, Charlie Williamson) . . . 'it is expected, I suppose, that some things might occur in it which would be out of the ordinary'."

Mary Eggleston continues: "Mary Louise presently lives alone in the house. Two previous tenants who have lived in the home moved away because of ghosts. Mary Louise and Charlie courageously stayed in the home, being interested and curious of the mysterious ghost. They have experienced a series of strange incidents during the 16 years they have lived there." Following are excerpted highlights of these happenings.

** In the fall of 1963, "The full moon made it possible to see objects very clearly. Mary Louise was sleeping on her good ear, but something woke her. She saw a figure of a man enter their room from the door on the right, walk across the room, and exit through the door on the left. He proceeded down a short hallway and disappeared from sight. Having much time to examine him, she described him as 'a servant in colonial times . . . a full shirt and baggy trousers all seemed to be a light color. The sleeves of his shirt were gathered in at the wrists, and his hair was white and cut, seemingly, in sort of a bob-type haircut.'

"Thinking Charlie had gone to the bathroom, she thought it was he, however, when she looked in his bed, which was next to hers, she found him in it — sound asleep!"

** On another occasion, Charlie saw the figure of a woman slip into the kitchen. He assumed it was his wife, Mary Louise. He called to her but she did not answer. He then looked in the kitchen. There was no one there. He then searched the living room and in the front yard. Nothing. He finally found Mary Louise in the bedroom — upstairs! She had been asleep for an hour. Who then had he seen?

** The couple had three German Shepherd dogs. According to Charlie: "Each one has apparently been able to see something that we have not been able to see, and to hear something that we haven't been able to hear." Mary Eggleston: "Lying in front of them, the (dog) would be sound asleep while Mary Louise and Charlie read or watched television. Suddenly, the dog's head would rise, growls would emerge from deep within his throat, and the fur surrounding his neck would bristle. His attention would be directed toward the ceiling above the piano, located on the left side of the living room. For a few moments, the dog would mysteriously watch something on the ceiling, then follow it down and over into the dining room. Cautiously, he would tip-toe toward the dining room and peek around the love seat. He would go no farther though, unless Mary Louise and Charlie would advance with him."

** On a cold night, Mary Louise, unable to sleep, decided to go downstairs, build a fire, and write some letters. She got a shovel and cleaned the fireplace of ashes, put them in a bag and placed in on the hearth. She then laid a fire with paper, kindling, small pieces of wood and a large log. She did not light the fire, however. By this time she felt sleepy, went upstairs and slept soundly.

The next morning she came back down to light the fire and

write her letters. She was astounded to find that instead of the kindling and logs, there were only ashes in the fireplace. Yet the bag of ashes she had filled the night before was still there on the hearth!

** Mary Eggleston: "Returning from an outing, Mary Louise and Charlie ascended the stairs to go to bed. Undressing, Mary Louise placed her black undergarment across her pocketbook. The next morning, Mary Louise picked the slip up to put it away." Here, Mary Louise is quoted: "The strap of the slip was inside the handle strap of the pocketbook. The threads, the original threads that were on the slip at both ends, I mean the straps of the slip at both ends, were intact. They were just as they were when they were bought from the store. To have gotten into the strap of the pocketbook, the slip would have had to have gone through a metal ring and then a leather opening before it could get into the inside of the strap of the pocketbook." Mary Eggleston adds that people from NASA, William and Mary College, and Colonial Williamsburg came "to see this amazing proof of a strange inhabitant. I personally have seen this phenomenon. I saw no evidence of broken seams in either the pocketbook or the slip!"

** Of all the eerie encounters Mary Louise and Charlie experienced over the years while living in the Cole Digges house, perhaps the most frightening occurred to Mary Louise on a hot summer night in 1963. Charlie was out of town. As she walked toward the dining room door she became enveloped in some sort of ethereal encasing. Here is how she described it: "My face, shoulder and arm became enwrapped in a flimsy, filmy sort of material, like fine veiling, or, I thought at the time, a curtain of cobwebs like you would see in an old barn. My face was covered so that it gave me a sort of smothered feeling!" She turned the light on, but saw nothing.

Such an experience would terrify most people, but Mary Louise apparently accepted it calmly, and both she and Charlie seemed unafraid of their resident spirit or spirits. Here is how Mary Eggleston quoted her great aunt on this: "You're afraid to believe what you wish about these happenings. . . Something does happen, for it happens to others. People often ask us if we're afraid to live here, or if we mind living here with these ghosts. We always tell them no, that we think it's rather interesting, and I hope that another time I have contact with one that I will be able to say something to it and maybe have a conversation. But anyway, we're looking forward to our next experience with them."

THE GHOST COACH OF BLACK SWAMP

he screams are still heard occasionally. And the spectral outline of the horse-driven carriage, hurtling into oblivion, is briefly glimpsed before it dematerializes! Such is the legend of the mystery of Black Swamp.

According to the most popular versions of this tale, the daughter of Governor Edward Digges was returning home late one night in her carriage, accompanied by her lady-in-waiting, an escort, and the driver. She had been to a party at the Yorktown Inn and was on the way home to Bellfield Plantation, traveling along the Old Williamsburg Road in York County, which some historians say is the oldest road in the country. George Washington used it on his way to the final surrender in Yorktown.

As the horses galloped through land which is now part of the Naval Weapons Station, something frightened them in the woods and they raced off, out of control, plowing head-long into a quagmire called the Black Swamp. The riders' terrified screams were muffled, as the dark, muddy quicksand swallowed them all, including the coach, without leaving a trace.

Although the Weapons Station officially denies it, there have been persistent stories of military men hearing the screams recurring in that murky area, and catching fleeting glances of the ill-fated coach sinking. In fact, the reports go back to the 1920s, when mention of the sightings was made in the Navy Mine Depot's official log.

In more recent years, a government spokesperson did tell a newspaper reporter that although he had not personally experienced the phenomenon, and there was no physical evidence to support it, that "there have been so many reports, some of them must be true." And if young Miss Digges, her lady-in-waiting, the escort and the driver did not vanish in Black Swamp on that fateful night many years ago, the key question remains unanswered: what did happen to them?

CHAPTER 22

Who Haunts Cornwallis' Cave?

ere it not for the intervention of fate, relatively few people would ever have heard of the sleepy little town of Yorktown, Virginia. But what transpired there for a few days in the middle of October 1781, etched Yorktown indelibly in the annals of American history. It was here, on the banks of the York River that General George Washington and his allies trapped the British army of Lord George Cornwallis, surrounded them, laid relentless cannon siege to the town, and forced a surrender that led to independence for the beleaguered American colonies.

The Revolutionary War had droned on for six years, and before this fretful lapse of military strategy on Cornwallis' part, there appeared to be no end of hostilities in immediate sight. Washington's rag tag army, half starved and ill clothed, was in danger of falling apart. Meanwhile, Cornwallis had stormed through the Carolinas with his elite corps. But as he marched northward he made the fateful decision to camp at Yorktown, believing the British Navy would fully support him by commanding the York River.

When Washington and his allies realized this, he saw an unprecedented opportunity to hem the British in, and with the support of French admiral Comte de Grasse, who with his ships beat the British to the river, Washington moved quickly. Nearly 9,000 Americans were joined by 8,000 Frenchmen, and they formed an impenetrable ring around Cornwallis and his 6,000 soldiers. The great allied bombardment began at 3 p.m. on October 9. In a curious twist of irony, American general Thomas Nelson was asked to "point out a good target toward which the artillerists could direct their fire." Stoically and without hesitation, he pointed to a large brick mansion which he suggested might be serving as Cornwallis' headquarters. The house Nelson indicated was his own! It was a magnificent act of patriotic self sacrifice which greatly impressed the Marquis de Lafayette and others. For several days the little town was shelled unmercifully. American and French cannons and mortars roared at full blast. American doctor James Thacher, a front line observer, wrote of the effect: "The haze of a soft Virginia fall day was thickened by welling cannon smoke, by the geysers of loose red dirt thrown skyward. . . " He figured at least 100 guns were at work. "The whole peninsula trembles under the incessant thunderings of our infernal machines. . . We are so near as to have a distinct view of the dreadful havoc and destruction of their works, and even see the men in their lines torn to pieces by the bursting of our shells."

Cornwallis was professional soldier enough to write to the British authority, on October 14: "My situation now becomes very critical. We dare not show a gun to their old batteries, and I expect that their new ones will open tomorrow morning . . . The safety of the place is, therefore, so precarious that I cannot recommend that the fleet and army should run great risque in endeavoring to save us."

In a move of great desperation, on the night of October 16, Cornwallis made a bold attempt to escape the trap. His plan was to try and cross the York River with as many able men as possible, leaving the wounded behind, fight his way through French troops at Gloucester Point, and proceed north to reunite with other British forces. Wrote Dr. Thacher: "A more preposterous and desperate attempt can scarcely be imagined. Boats were secretly prepared, arrangements made, and a large proportion of his troops actually embarked . . ."

Then fate struck again. Dr. Thacher: "From a moderate and calm evening, a most violent storm of wind and rain ensued. The boats with the remaining troops were all driven down the river, and it was not till the next day that his troops could be returned to the garrison at York." Many soldiers drowned.

Cornwallis now knew that he was doomed. There was no escape. Then, at 10 a.m. on October 17, a strange sight appeared when the fog and smoke of the guns rose from the fields. A red-jacketed little British drummer boy appeared above the haze standing atop a parapet. As the firing ceased, the clear sound of the beat of his drum was heard. It was a signal to halt the battle. As one American officer wrote: "I never heard a drum equal to it — the most delightful music to us all."

The surrender was sealed on October 19, 1781, thus, in effect, ending the war and ensuring American independence.

There are many ghostly overtones at Yorktown, attributable to the historic fight that took place there. Tourists have reported seeing apparitional soldiers appear on the battlefields. The sounds of booming cannons have been heard by visitors more than 200 years after they roared incessantly at Yorktown. There is, allegedly, the ghost of a trapped British soldier in the Nelson House at Yorktown, and there is another spirit who is said to haunt the Moore House, across the battlefields, where the terms of surrender were signed.

And there are also suspected supernatural "happenings" at a

Cornwallis' cave

natural tunnel-like opening on the banks of the York River histori-cally known as Cornwallis' Cave. This cavity of 12 by 18 feet, known to have existed at least as far back as the 18th century, may well have been a smugglers' hideout in pirating days. There is another theory that the excavation was enlarged during the siege of Yorktown by townspeople who took refuge there, and hid their valuables as the shells blasted all around them. It also has long been rumored that General Cornwallis himself, and members of his staff, scurried to the cave to escape the intensity of the shellings, although there is no definitive proof of this. He may, in fact, have sought another dug out haven a quarter of a mile away.

Regardless of the difficulty of separating fact from legend, however, the cave stands today on the embankment and is closed off at the entrance by a barred gate. One can only peek in now and see a few feet inside. For at least the last half century or so, some Yorktown residents insist that there is something in there, possibly something evil. Here again, there are differing hypotheses as to what it might be.

Foreboding sounds seem to emanate from inside the cave, especially at night. They have been variously described as men talking or whispering, groans, moaning, and "incantations." A number of people, both visitors and residents alike, have reported hearing them. Since the cave has been closed for years, no one has been able (perhaps no one wanted to) to venture inside and investigate.

Some believe they are the voices of the spirits of long-dead British soldiers who sought shelter here. But there also is a persis-tent feeling that the "voices" may be of a more recent origin. Years ago, before the cave was gated, it was said that a group of "devil worshipers" used the place to hold Satanic rituals. Many feel that is a plausible answer to the incantations heard there.

Two Hampton residents who have not only heard these eerie sounds, but have tape recorded them, are Belinda and Richard Thomas. Both are amateur ghost hunters who track haunting leg-ends with their recorders and cameras. "It definitely is what I would call 'a power place'," says Belinda. "We have photographs showing a vortex in there." She describes a vortex as being a place where spirits can move in and out. "When we went there, we stuck the tape recorder inside the bars of the gate, and we definitely got some strange sounds," Belinda says. (The author has heard the sounds and seen the photographs, and they are, while not conclu-sive that ghosts exist in the cave, still, intriguing and impressive.)

"We believe they are chantings, but, of course, the sounds are open to interpretation," she concludes.

"I stuck my hands inside the bars and took some photos with my camera one night," Richard adds. "I was scared. I definitely sensed something in there."

The National Park Service, which operates the Yorktown Battlefield, has no official comment on Cornwallis' Cave. They refuse to speculate on the ethereal sounds so many people have reportedly heard there.

The entrance to the cave is a forbidding sight, and . . . who knows?

CHAPTER 23

An Exorcism (or two)
at the Nelson House

(Author's note: At the historic Nelson House in Yorktown, I wrote, in Volume I, about the ghost of a British soldier who was killed there during the last days of the Revolutionary War. Built in the early 1700s, the house was owned by Thomas Nelson during the war. He was a member of the Continental Congress, Commanding General of the Virginia militia, a governor of the commonwealth, and a signer of the Declaration of Independence.

It was Nelson, who directed artillery fire on his own home during the siege of Yorktown, when British officers were using it as a headquarters. The results of the cannon fire can still be seen in the walls. Off limits to visitors today is a secret stairway hidden behind a panel in the dining room hall leading to a garret. According to local legend a British soldier hiding here in October 1781, was killed by a blast. Through the years he has occasionally made his presence known.

Perhaps the most frightening encounter occurred to a Mrs. Blow, who lived in the house in the early 1900s. She was hosting a luncheon one day when one of her guests inquired about the resident spirit. Mrs. Blow said she had not seen or heard anything out of the ordinary.

At that precise moment the secret door behind the panel in the dining room burst open with a "terrific force" that shook the room as if an earthquake had hit. "Something" then crashed into the sideboard with such violence "that several dishes crashed to the floor, shattered beyond repair." Although the ladies were obvious-

Nelson House

ly terrified at the poltergeist-type manifestation, Mrs. Blow said it must have been caused by a sudden down draft of air. No one really believed her.

In 1990, Nelson Farley of Newport News, a descendent of the Nelson family, visited the house of his ancestors. A keen student of the paranormal, and a self-styled psychic, Farley, who has exchanged ghost lore with me, told of the following:)

hen he and his friend, Barbara Smith, toured, they were told by a guide of a young Yankee soldier who had died there when the house was used as a Union hospital during the Civil War. The soldier fell in love with his nurse, and, the guide said, his ghost still resides in the attic.

Farley then felt a strong desire to "help" the spirit, to "release" him from his present location so he could perhaps rejoin his beloved nurse. So he and Barbara arranged to come back to the house one morning before it was open to tourists. Farley was allowed access to the attic. "I had no idea what to expect," he says, "let alone what danger might be involved."

Farley then spoke to the unseen entity: "I understand you were in love with a nurse here, but you died. From what I'm told, she loved you, too. There is such a thing as reincarnation, where people return to the earth after some spiritual preparation. . . I can't see anything keeping you two apart, but you won't get with her by staying up in this attic. Any lady would feel lucky to have a man who thought enough of her to grieve up here for 125 years. Look around you and see your father, mother, brothers, sisters, or friends ready to accompany you to the spirit world."

Farley then questioned himself as to whether he had accomplished anything. "I then felt a strong energy glow inside me," he recalls. "It was warm, loving, and expressed 'thank you' clearly enough."

Next, Farley went downstairs to the door of the secret room and addressed the ghost of the British soldier. "The colonies and Britain are now friends," he said. "It is 1990; you have been in that passage over 200 years. It does you no good; you need to go to the spirit world to develop." As with the Civil War soldier, Farley directed the Britisher to follow his relatives and friends who would guide him.

Several days later, Farley says the ghost appeared to him, still dressed in his red coat. Why was he still here, Farley questioned. Then he thought that since the soldier had died so long ago, perhaps his relatives were no longer "available." So Farley asked several deceased members of his own family if they would come to lead the soldier. "I immediately had a peaceful reassuring feeling that this was what he needed," Farley said.

Neither ghost has appeared at Nelson House since.

CHAPTER 24

The Jealous Barkeep of Yorktown

ittle did Margaret Thompson know what lay ahead of her when she moved into the old medical shop in Yorktown in 1981. After all, she was excited, and justifiably so. She was now to reside in the heart of the town's historic section, and she was within easy walking distance of her office at the National Park Service. She loved her job as a park officer, and everything appeared to be going her way. Margaret, for the moment at least, was at peace with the world.

The serenity lasted only a few months, however. Then all hell broke loose. "It started with the flowers," the attractive, effervescent Margaret says. "I love flowers. I had put all kinds of flowers in the house, most of them in glass jars, and I had placed them on the deep window sills. Well, I came home from work one evening, and the flowers, jars and all, were thrown at me. They were literally thrown at me! And there was no one else in the house. Needless to say, it unnerved me. I have a degree in science — biology — so I was looking for a rational explanation. There had to be one. But I couldn't find it.

"That was the first experience I had with the presence that came to be an intimate if not always welcome part of my life for the next four years," Margaret says. Whatever it was, it made itself known in a number of different ways. "I would hear footsteps in the attic late at night, yet I knew no one was there," she adds. "I had a double dead-bolt lock on the front and back doors. There was no way for anyone to get in, yet the footsteps were very distinct. And every time I would search for the source, I found nothing.

"I would leave some lights on when I went to sleep and when I woke up the entire house would be in darkness. The lights had all been turned out. And then there were the cold spots. Usually they were around the fireplace, or by my bed, or in the bathroom. You could move just a few feet, from one spot to another, and the temperature seemed to drop 10 to 20 degrees. Then if you took a few steps to the other side, you would be out of it. It was weird."

Perplexed, Margaret told some co-workers about her experiences, and some stayed with her in the house. Nothing ever happened while they were there, and they began giving Margaret strange looks. "People kept telling me I was just nervous and imagining things," she remembers. "Hell, I don't have a nervous bone in my body. They began to think I was crazy, so I stopped telling anybody about it."

The occurrences continued. The ghost seemed to be playful at times, and would hide or misplace Margaret's clothes and personal items. She would search for days for things only to find them out in the open in places where they hadn't been before. Once her mother, Elizabeth Thompson of Richmond, came over for a visit. "She always wore a special pair of flat shoes when she drove," Margaret says. "So when she arrived we placed the shoes on the attic steps. A few days later when she was ready to leave, the shoes were gone. We looked everywhere, but we couldn't find them. They had disappeared. She drove back to Richmond and I followed her in my car. When we got there, we walked into the kitchen, and there were her driving shoes, sitting on top of the kitchen table!"

Margaret's mother had two other brushes with the 'presence' while she was visiting her daughter at Yorktown. On one occasion, she clearly heard the sounds of heavy breathing coming from the fireplace area. On another, a camera's flash attachment exploded on a table near the fireplace. Mrs. Thompson couldn't explain such happenings, but she refused to believe they had anything to do with the supernatural.

At times Margaret would see her rocking chair rock by itself. Her kitten would sometimes slap a paw and leap at an imaginary string, as if it was being dangled by an unseen hand. And there were the odors; powerful odors. "There were three distinct ones," Margaret says. One was wintergreen, and one was Resonil, which is an old-time salve used for such things as scraped knees.

Margaret described the third smell as that of a musty old vacuum cleaner bag, which she says is a "standard other world odor." These smells would come and go, as if they were directly associated with the ghost.

As time went on, Margaret began to sense that it was a male spirit and "he" was jealous. It seemed that every time she had a date, if he didn't like the date, he would make his displeasure known. Light fuses would blow inexplicably. Keys would be lost. Items of clothing would be missing, and when there was real irritation, dishes would be smashed and the whole house would be torn apart.

"He" particularly didn't like Margaret's square dance partner. "In square dancing you have matching costumes, down to the handkerchief," she explains. "It's a very precise ensemble, and on nights when I was supposed to go dancing, I couldn't find certain parts of the outfit. So I couldn't go on those nights. Usually, the next day they would surface. It was very frustrating."

Even more bothersome were the times when Margaret would come home from a date to find her house ransacked. "Dishes were all over the floor, and it looked like every drawer in the house had been turned upside down and the contents dumped out," she says. "I really got mad. I cussed at 'him.' I told him I was tired of cleaning up after him." It got so bad, she bought a set of plastic dishes. On one or two occasions she even witnessed objects rising off tables and sailing through the air.

Twice, Margaret caught fleeting glimpses of her spirit. Once, she saw a "flash of white" in the kitchen. The other time, on Yorktown Day, she caught the reflection of a man's shoulder in her mirror. He was clothed in white and had a "blousy-type" sleeve reminiscent of colonial garb. "I thought someone had gotten into the house and I yelled at him to get out," Margaret says. "But when I turned around to face the mirror there was no one there. I was told later that he wouldn't fully materialize in front of me because there was not enough positive kinetic energy. Since I was not a true believer, there were some 'unfavorable vibes' which held him back."

After a period of several months of intermittent occurrences, the combination of curiosity and frustration got to Margaret. If she were going to continue to be haunted, she wanted to know something about who was doing the haunting and why. Friends suggested she contact an area medium who had a reputation for contacting spirits from "the other world." A seance was set up in

Margaret Thompson

Margaret's house. The attendees were Margaret, the medium, and two "friendlies," who were described as people with positive vibes which help bring out spirits.

The seance proved both informative and eventful. "We heard pacing in the attic," Margaret recalls. "There were the sounds of someone going up and down the stairs, and doors being scratched. There was a big-leafed plant in the room and the leaves bent as if they were being blown by a high wind. The place where the medium sat got as cold as ice, although I was sitting just across the room from her and I was hot.

"The medium said the spirit was in the room with us. She said he was a white male of British lineage from a noble family. He was the second or third son, who had been sent to America more than 200 years ago in disgrace. He was in his 30s, over six feet tall and had dark hair and dark eyes and a full beard. He spoke with a French accent, and he had a badly healed duel wound on his right palm. This possibly explained the odors of wintergreen and Resonil."

The medium said his name was Robert Queasly Baker and that

he was very romantic and considered himself a poet. She said he worked in Yorktown during the time of the Revolutionary War in a tavern. "That fit perfectly," Margaret says, "because the medical shop where I lived had been built over the foundation of an old tavern of that period."

The woman said Robert had fought in the battle of Yorktown and had later become destitute, fell ill and died from a disease and was buried in an unmarked grave in the pauper's cemetery in Yorktown. "There was a pauper's cemetery just as she described it," Margaret says, "but the medium had been in town for just a week or two, and I am sure she had no way of knowing about it."

The medium went on. The reason Robert was "with" Margaret was the fact that they had been lovers in the 18th century. He had been a barkeep and she had been a bar maid, a wench "of loose morals." He retained a romantic interest in her and was very protective. This explained his jealous rages when she went out on dates.

The medium then talked about the cold spots in the house. This was Robert. Whenever he was present there would be a cold spot, generally by Margaret's bed, in her bathroom, or by the fireplace with which, the woman said, he was somehow associated. At the end of the seance, the medium asked Robert to leave the house, and within minutes there was a sharp slamming of the front door.

Afterwards, Margaret did some detective work. She verified that there had been an old tavern on the site, and that there was a pauper's cemetery on Read Street, now hidden under a paved parking lot. She found the name Robert Queasly Baker in colonial records. His appearance was substantiated some time later by the Yorktown visit of a 300-pound psychic who told her that Robert did indeed have piercing black eyes, with flaming dark red hair and beard, "Like that of a Viking." The psychic was in town to investigate a ghost in the Moore House, and nearly died in the effort. While walking up the stairs in the house he collapsed and said he was suffocating, he couldn't breathe. Margaret helped revive him.

After the seance, Robert's activities diminished somewhat, although he still kicked up a fuss when he became upset. For example, in October 1982, Margaret agreed to be interviewed for a newspaper article about her ghost if the writer would not reveal her name or where she lived. When she met the reporter, Margaret told her, "I had a hard time getting out of the house this morning. All the fuses were blowing, my appliances wouldn't work, and my clothes were out of place. He's not very happy about this story."

On at least two occasions Robert, who Margaret says often traveled with her, was inadvertently left behind when she returned home. Uncomfortable in strange surroundings, he created mild forms of havoc which brought pleas to Margaret to "get him out of here." Once, for example, she visited her mother in Richmond during the year-end holiday season, and then returned home. Hardly had she arrived when her mother, irate, called. Why, she wanted to know, had Margaret stuffed Christmas cookies deep down into the recesses of her sofa?

"You have to understand that nobody goes into my mother's living room unless she is having special guests," Margaret says. "I told her I hadn't been near the room and that I certainly wouldn't cram cookies in the couch. I said it must be Robert. He must have gotten left behind. She nearly panicked. She wanted me to get him out of there, so I yelled through the phone for Robert to leave. Mother told me later that night after she hung up, she heard the front door slam. I guess Robert didn't want to stay where he wasn't wanted."

On the other occasion, Robert got left behind at the volunteer fire station on Hubbard Lane in Williamsburg. Margaret served as an emergency medical technician, certified in CPR, at the station a few years ago, and sometimes, it seemed, Robert went with her. They even "talked" to him through a Ouija board. This particular time, Margaret left the station to go home and the firemen put a big pot of water on the stove to make a batch of spaghetti, only the water wouldn't boil. They called Margaret and she ordered Robert to leave. Within minutes the firemen heard one of their exterior doors slam shut, and simultaneously, the water on the stove began to boil.

As a sidelight, Margaret says that through Robert during an Ouija session, the volunteers found out their station was built on or very close to an old Indian graveyard. In fact, Robert told them about one of the Indians, an old squaw named Severette. It was she, the firemen believed, who once left a woman's footprints in the dust of the loft in the station house. That the place had spirits of its own became more certain in Margaret's mind one night when she came in to pull her shift. She found that a Bible had been placed on every bunk in the building, but no one would tell her why.

"I couldn't get anyone to talk," she recalls. "They all were as white as sheets. Something had obviously scared them." Finally, the truth came out. The volunteers had been playing with the Ouija board when they "conjured up the Devil." They said they looked at one of the windows, which was set up high off the ground, and they saw the image of Satan himself looking down upon them. That's when they had gotten out the Bibles and that's all Margaret could get out of them. No one wanted to talk any more about it.

As time wore on, Robert's appearances became less frequent. In 1984, Margaret left the National Park Service and moved to Williamsburg. Since then he has not thrown any tantrums. In fact, he has been eerily silent. "I feel he is still there. He's still protecting me," Margaret says. "I know he'll never harm me. Now, he doesn't feel I need him as much."

More recently, Margaret went to another psychic and had more readings. From these she was told that she and Robert actually had been together in three different lifetimes. One in Yorktown, one during Christ's time on earth, and one in ancient Egyptian times. Perhaps that explains why Margaret, when asked the question if she would be relieved if Robert ever left for good, answered, "I'd never believe he was really gone. I've got him for life."

The Further Spectral Returns of Miss Evelyn Byrd

One thing that sets Evelynton, on Route 5, adjacent to Westover Church, halfway between Williamsburg and Richmond, apart from most of the other well-known plantations nearby is its age. It is just a little more than 60 years old. In the 1930s, Duncan Lee, the noted architect responsible for the restoration of Carter's Grove, was commissioned to design a Georgian Revival manor house atop the original foundation. Constructed of 250 year old brick, it is considered a brilliant interpretation of the style, and has been lovingly restored and furnished with American, English and continental antiques, many of them family heirlooms.

Actually, the present house is the third one to be built on the crest of a ridge which overlooks both the James River and Westover. The first one was an overseer's home and no one is quite sure when it was built. It was there when Edmund Ruffin, Jr., bought the original plantation site of 860 acres at an auction in 1847.

His father, Edmund Ruffin, has been described in an Evelynton brochure as being "one of the South's most colorful figures". He was, certainly, flamboyant, irascible, and a violently outspoken advocate of state's rights and secession. One biographer said he was "fanatical in his hatred of the North, had long predicted war (between the states), preached disunion, handed out pamphlets,

Evelyn Byrd

and had encouraged ladies' shooting clubs to prepare Southern women to defend themselves during the conflict."

He also was known as an eccentric genius and has been called the father of American agronomy. His early scientific innovations, based on the discovery of marl as a neutralizer for Virginia's highly acidic soil, rescued the state's declining agricultural economy in the early 19th century.

But Ruffin was probably best known for a single feat. Because of his zealous advocacy of Southern supremacy, he was accorded the honor, at age 66, of firing the first shot of the Civil War at Fort Sumter, South Carolina, in 1861; a fact that came back to haunt Evelynton.

A year later the plantation site played a minor, although interesting role that, but for fate, could have had a devastating effect on General George McClellan's Peninsula campaign and may have altered the entire course of the war. It is known as the battle of Evelynton Heights, and occurred on the rainy morning of July 3, 1862, two days after the bloody fight at Malvern Hill a few miles to the west. There, column after column of courageous Confederate infantryman were murderously mowed down by rows of Union artillery placed at a commanding position at the crest of a hill.

Despite his decisive victory, the cautious-to-a-fault McClellan ordered a retreat back to Harrison's Landing at Berkeley Plantation on the James River. There he pitched camp to rest and regroup his fatigued army of 100,000. But, through an oversight, one of the Union flanks — at Evelynton Heights — was left unprotected.

The men of the charismatic Confederate cavalryman, J.E.B. Stuart, took this strategic point and set up a single howitzer. It was all they had. And here, Stuart miscalculated. He had anticipated being joined by thousands of troops under the commands of generals Stonewall Jackson and James Longstreet. But Jackson's men were exhausted and mired in mud and didn't arrive until the next day. Longstreet's army took a wrong turn and was six miles away when Stuart had his lone cannon and some erratic congreve rockets, fire on McClellan's encampment.

The unexpected shelling caused considerable alarm, but only minimal damage. Stuart's men were soon routed from the heights by superior forces. By the time Jackson arrived on July 4th, the Federal forces were too entrenched to be removed. Some historians have speculated that had Jackson and Longstreet gotten there in time, the entire Army of the Potomac might have been lost, or at the least, heavy casualties, not to mention loss of prestige, might have resulted.   Possibly because of the embarrassment to the Union at Evelynton Heights, but much more likely because of the Federal hatred of Edmund Ruffin, the house there was burned to the ground and the fields were laced with salt. The plantation lay in ruins for years.

Evelynton originally belonged to William Byrd II of Westover. He had intended to give it to his lovely daughter, Evelyn, when she married, but this was not to be.

She died before reaching 30. On her tombstone was inscribed

the following: "Here in the sleep of peace reposes the body of Evelyn Byrd, daughter of the Honorable William Byrd. The various and excellent endowments of nature: improved and perfected by an accomplished education formed her, for happiness of her friends; for the ornament of her country. Alas Reader! We can detail nothing, however valued, from unrelenting death. Beauty, fortune, or valued honour! So here a proof! And be reminded by this awful tomb that every worldly comfort fleets away. Excepting only, what arises from imitating the virtues of our friends and the contemplation of their happiness. To which, God was pleased to call this Lady on the 13th day of November, 1737, in the 29th year of her age."

Months later, Evelyn's closest friend in life, Anne Harrison of neighboring Berkeley Plantation, was walking through a poplar

Miss Evelyn Byrd's Tomb

grove when she felt "a presence." She turned and saw a figure approaching. It was Evelyn. She was "dressed in white, dazzling in ethereal loveliness. She drifted forward a few steps, kissed her hand to the beholder, smiling happily, and vanished."

In the intervening generations, many others have caught fleeting glimpses of Evelyn, among them former Westover owners and guests. In December 1929, for example, a guest of the Richard Cranes, who then owned the plantation, reported seeing the "filmy, nebulous and cloudy figure of a woman, so transparent no features could be distinguished, only the gauzy texture of the woman's form." It seemed, the guest said, "to be floating a little above the lawn."

But of all who have claimed sightings of Evelyn at Westover, no one could offer a reasonable explanation as to why her restless spirit would want to periodically return to a place which apparently caused her so much unhappiness in life. Nor does it explain why she has reappeared, as recently as the 1990s, at Evelynton.

"We haven't seen her," says present plantation mistress Lisa Ruffin Harrison, "but I can tell you this. I have heard many stories of oldtimers in the area who claim to have seen her, and the peculiar thing about these reports is that they are all the same. They came from different people at different times, but they apparently all saw the same thing." Mrs. Harrison says that 40 or 50 years ago many long-time area residents used to come onto the property and fish in Herring Creek which leads into the James River.

"They all told of looking back at the house and seeing the silhouette of what they called 'an old fashioned lady' weeping into her handkerchief in an upstairs window," Mrs. Harrison states. She adds that a number of psychics have visited the house and grounds since they were reopened to the public in 1986. "Several of them said, with no prompting from us, that Evelyn's presence is definitely here. Some sensed it on the stairs, and others felt a strong sensation in the boxwood gardens." She also has been sighted on a high ridge overlooking the river and Westover.

Barbara Rand, who works at the plantation, has had the same experience. "We had a tour recently, and one of the women, who was a psychic, ran up to me and excitedly declared, 'She's here, she's here'," Mrs. Rand said. "The hair on the woman's arm was standing straight up."

Is it possible Evelyn Byrd returns in hopes of spiritually reuniting with her lost lover of more than 250 years ago?

When Evelyn Byrd died, an eloquent obituary notice was

placed in the area newspaper, the Virginia Gazette, in the issue of December 9, 1737. It read:

Ever constant to her Friend,
Vigilant in Truth's Defence;
Entertaining to her End,
Life! brimful of Eloquence,
Youth in Person; Age in Sense,
Nature gave her Store immense.
But she's fled, and is no more,
Yonder soars in Fields of Light!
Robbed of all our little Store,
Death! Oh Death! we're ruined quite!

(Author's note: Among the more intriguing letters I have gotten over past the few years was one from a young lady named Ann Smathers from Albuquerque, New Mexico, of all places. Her parents apparently had visited Williamsburg, Virginia, sometime during the summer and fall of 1992 and had taken Ann a copy of "The Ghosts of Tidewater."

So she wrote: "In your book you have a curious photograph on page 57 of the old mansion of Evelynton. Near the main door to the mansion there looks like a lady dressed in white and she appears to be sitting on the front porch. When, on page 61, you wrote, '. . .Nor does it explain why she (Evelyn Byrd) has reappeared, as recently as when this book was going to press, at Evelynton. . .' were you referring to that picture?

"I don't know for sure if I believe in ghosts or not, but I have never ruled out the possibility and I'm not offended if anyone ever suggests it to me. If you weren't talking about the picture, there could be many other explanations for what I see in it.

"It could be dust on the negative.

"There could be weird lighting.

"You, or whoever did the photograph, could have had someone there.

"It could be other things.

"It could be Evelyn Byrd."

Her letter fascinated me. Evelyn Byrd was a lady who allegedly died of a broken heart in the 18th century because her father would not let her marry the man she loved. She was only 29 when she departed this earth, and many claim she frequently returns not only to her home at Westover Plantation on Route 5 between Richmond and Williamsburg, but also to the mansion which has been named for her — Evelynton.

I had photographed the house in 1989 when I was doing research for "The Ghosts of Tidewater." I dug through dusty files in my storage room to find the original photograph, and sure enough, there was "something" on the porch of the house that I had not noticed before. I got a little excited.

Under a large magnifying glass, it appears that what is there may be a child or young girl, with blonde hair, with her back to the camera, dressed all in white. I didn't recall seeing anyone on the porch the day I took the picture, but it is possible there was a tourist or someone seated on a bench there.

But then again, if it isn't a person, who or what is it? Was Miss Evelyn Byrd playing tricks with me? Anyway, judge for yourself.

Evelynton — and the mysterious figure on the porch.

MISS EVELYN AND A GOSSAMER BUTTERFLY

(Author's note: As this book was ready to go to press, I received a letter from Martha Wilson of Farmville, North Carolina. She asked if I would send her some books for a charity auction she was chairing, which I gladly did. In the envelope was the photograph on the right, which she explained as follows:

Miss Evelyn

"Since becoming disabled several years ago, ghosts have become sort of a hobby with me. I started making them because my mother wanted some for Halloween one year, and the next thing I knew, I had a one-woman show full of them at the local arts council, and I had sold the little fabric sculptures to folks as far away as Sweden! I soon discovered that I really liked reading about historical ghosts and spirits, and I often incorporate their legends into my renditions.

"I am enclosing a picture of one of my little sculptures that was inspired by the ghost of Evelyn Byrd at Westover (and Evelynton). You may not be able to tell, but she is kneeling and holding a gossamer butterfly.")

The Haunting Dreams of William Byrd, II

illiam Byrd, II, was, by virtually all accounts, one of the most extraordinary men of his time (1674-1744). He was a brilliant colonist who owned Westover Plantation in Charles City County. He had a beautiful daughter, Evelyn Byrd, who allegedly died at a tender age of a broken heart when her father wouldn't let her marry the man she loved. She is said to return in ghostly form in and around the plantation.

William Byrd, II, could speak and read several languages, including English, Hebrew, Latin and Greek; had the best library of the times in Virginia; was a charismatic leader and public servant; and certainly one of the most educated and intelligent men of his era. Yet, he also seemed to have a sense for psychic activity. In the introduction to his book, "The Secret Diary of William Byrd of Westover," it states, "Although Byrd was in most respects a typical 18th century rationalist, he had a vein of superstition that comes out in his attitude toward dreams."

In this particular diary, one of three different volumes, the period of 1709 to 1712 is covered. Here are a few entries concerning dreams:

* April 8, 1709: "The Indian woman died this evening, according to a dream I had last night about her."

* July 15, 1709: "I had a bad dream this morning which seemed to foretell the death of some of my family. I thought I saw my yard full of people and when I came into the house I could not find my wife."

* March 31, 1710: "Mrs. Burwell dreamed this night that she

William Bryd, II

saw a person with money scales, weighed time, and declared that there was no more than 18 pennies worth of time to come, which seems to be a dream with some significance either concerning the world or a sick person."

* April 10, 1710: "I sent early to inquire after Mr. Harrison (of neighboring Berkeley Plantation) and received word that he died

about 4 o'clock this morning which completed the 18th day of his sickness, according to Mrs. Burwell's dream exactly. Just before his death he was sensible and desired (a woman in attendance), with importunity, to open the door because he wanted to go out and could not go till the door was open, and as soon as the door was opened he died."

* June 18, 1710: "In the afternoon my wife told me a dream she had two nights. She thought she saw a scroll in the sky in the form of a light cloud with writing on it. It ran extremely fast from west to east with great swiftness. The writing she could not read but there was a woman before her that told her there would be a great dearth because of want of rain and after that a pestilence for that the seasons were changed and time inverted."

* June 21, 1710: "About five nights since I dreamed I saw a flaming star in the air at which I was much frightened and called some others to see it but when they came it disappeared. I fear this portends some judgment to this country or at least to myself."

* July 21, 1710: "About eight nights ago I dreamed that several of my Negroes lay sick on the floor and one Indian among the rest, and now it came exactly to pass."

* December 31, 1710: "Some night this month I dreamed that I saw a flaming sword in the sky and called some company to see it but before they could come it disappeared, and about a week after my wife and I were walking and we discovered in the clouds a shining cloud exactly in the shape of a dart and seemed to be over my plantation but it soon disappeared likewise. Both these appearances seemed to foretell some misfortune to me which afterwards came to pass in the death of several of my Negroes after a very unusual manner.

"My wife about two months since dreamed she saw an angel in the shape of a big woman who told her the time was altered and the seasons were changed and that several calamities would follow that confusion. God avert his judgment from this poor country."

* January 6, 1711: "Poor old (name undeciphered) died this night to make up the number of the dead."

* January 16, 1712: "I dreamed a coffin was brought into my house and thrown into the hall."

* January 19, 1712: "I dreamed a mourning coach drove into my garden and stopped at the house door."

It is noted that two of William Byrd's four children by his first wife, Lucy Parke Byrd, did not survive infancy, and Lucy herself died at an early age in 1716.

CHAPTER 27

Bizarre Happenings at Berkeley

But for an ironic quirk of fate, the U.S. may have lost two future presidents and one signer of the Declaration of Independence, and thus the course of American history might have been dramatically altered — all in the flash of a single lightning bolt. And therein lies a tale of interest, intrigue and psychic phenomena that remains unexplained to this day.

It happened on a dark rainy night in 1744. As the storm gathered fury sweeping up the James River, Benjamin Harrison, IV, master of Berkeley Plantation in Charles City County, halfway between Richmond and Williamsburg, dashed through the house closing windows and locking shutters. In an upstairs bedroom overlooking the river, he apparently had trouble with a particular window which seemed to be stuck. He called for help, and two of his daughters came to his aid.

As they stood silhouetted in the window, a terrific flash of lightning struck them, killing all but Benjamin Harrison, IV, who died later after being bled by a physician. Benjamin Harrison, V, however, was not present at the window, and grew to become a leader of the American Colonies, signed the Declaration of Independence, and sired William Henry Harrison, who distinguished himself as an Indian fighter, earning the name "Tippecanoe," and later was elected ninth President of the United States. His grandson, another Benjamin Harrison, became 23rd President of the United States.

It is said that the ghosts of Benjamin Harrison, IV, and at least one of his daughters have never left Berkeley; that their "presence," in the form of peculiar manifestations, is still regularly felt by the residents, staff members and even visitors to the plantation. More on this later.

First, it is noteworthy to consider the rich historical lore that surrounds Berkeley, which has been described as the finest mansion among the many that dot historic Route 5 linking Richmond and Williamsburg.

The plantation land itself was part of a grant made in 1619 by King James I to the Berkeley Company and was designated "Berkeley And Hundred." There is controversy surrounding the arrival of the first settlers to this area. In contrast to what many history books report, Virginians are adamant in believing that the first actual observance of Thanksgiving was, in fact, held at Berkeley in 1619, two years before the Pilgrims celebrated in New England.

According to Dr. Samuel E. Burr, Jr., a retired university history professor, Captain John Woodlief left Bristol, England on September 15, 1619, and reached Berkeley Plantation early in December. "On December 4, 1619," says Dr. Burr, "the crew held a Thanksgiving observance. Although many of their number had died during their first year in America, there had been a bountiful harvest, and it seemed right to give thanks for this to a merciful God.

"These English settlers were joined by about 90 American Indians, led by their Chief Massasoit," notes Dr. Burr. "There were religious services — also military drills, games of skill, singing and sumptuous feast." He says the menu consisted of turkeys, venison, bear meat, greens, herbs, ducks, geese, shellfish, eels, codfish, flounder, wild fruit and berries and a variety of wines and "home brew." He adds that cranberries and pumpkin pies were not added until years later.

It is likely such services, as an annual event, did not last long, however, for it was at Berkeley, on Good Friday, 1622, that a band of marauding Indians stormed the fragile settlement and killed nine people. For years afterward, the 8,000 or so acres of Berkeley Hundred were abandoned.

The site was not reclaimed until 1636. It eventually became the property of John Bland, a merchant of London. His son, Giles Bland, was a favored lieutenant of the rebellion leader, Nathanial Bacon, and when Bacon's insurrection collapsed in 1676, Bland was ordered hanged by, coincidentally, Governor Sir William Berkeley.

The property then came into the possession of Benjamin Harrison III, whose ancestors were from Wakefield. His son, Benjamin, IV, built the Georgian style, three-story brick mansion in 1726.

Incidentally, in addition to claiming the first official

Berkeley

Thanksgiving, Berkeley also is listed as being the site of the first commercial shipyard, and, in 1621, of having the first bourbon whiskey distilled there. Further distinctions include the fact that every United States President from George Washington through John Tyler (the 10th) was entertained by the gracious hospitality of the plantation's hosts. Washington, a close friend of Benjamin Harrison, V, often visited.

There are dubious glories associated with the plantation, too. It was ransacked during the Revolutionary War by Benedict Arnold. During the early years of the Civil War, General McClelland used the house as headquarters for his Army of the Potomac as he battled with Robert E. Lee in his attempts to march on Richmond. Lincoln visited his general there, and at one time there were as many as 140,000 Union troops in the area. It is said the cellar once was used as a prison for Confederate soldiers.

Today, visitors can see Civil War bullets with toothmarks in them where soldiers bit while being operated on. The house was converted to a hospital. And, it was at Berkeley, in July 1862, that Union General Daniel Butterfield composed the classic military strains of "Taps."

It was also during the Civil War that a 14-year-old drummer boy first saw Berkeley. His name was John Jamieson. In the latter years of the war, the house was abused badly, at one point being turned into an animal barn. It lay in disrepair for decades. Jamieson subsequently became a successful engineer, and, 50 years after he had first been there, came back to buy the ruined plantation. His son, Malcolm "Mac" Jamieson moved to Berkeley in 1930, and he and his wife, Grace, devoted their lives to restoring the place to its original grandeur.

Thus, today, Berkeley is a lovely place to visit. From the front of the house, five terraces, dug during the Revolutionary War, lead to the James River. Boxwood gardens flank the path, which meets with a ladies winter garden of roses and other flowers. Inside, the restored rooms are furnished with Queen Anne secretaries, English Hepplewhite clocks, a 1725 gentleman's chest, and a 1690 William and Mary chest from Scotland, in addition to fine paintings and portraits. The house is open to the public and expert guides retell its rich history daily.

Ah, but what of the ghosts?

The late Mac Jamieson said one of the most common manifestations was that the balky bedroom window, where Benjamin Harrison, IV, and his daughters stood when they were struck by lightning, periodically slammed shut by itself, as if closed by unseen hands.

"For no apparent reason that window sometimes will close by itself," Jamieson said. "I was in the room one day and was telling a friend about the legend, when the window began to come down while we were looking at it. Now," he laughs, "everybody accuses me of having a button that I push to make the window close, which I haven't, of course."

Others have reported sighting the apparition of a young girl with an infant in her arms at the window late at night. Investigations have revealed no one upstairs at the time.

Mac also told of the legend of the "ghost in the bottom." He says there is a dip in the road leading into the mansion, and for centuries it has been believed to be haunted by a young child who cries at night. Jamieson was skeptical of this story, however. "Personally, I think it probably was an owl, but the plantation owners didn't discourage the story because it tended to keep the slaves in their quarters at night rather than out partying. The owners felt this kept the slaves fresh for a day's work the next morning so they let the tale perpetuate itself."

There is no logical explanation, however, for the plight of a poor photographer who once visited the plantation. First, he took still pictures. One was of the portrait of Mrs. Jamieson's third great grandmother, Elizabeth Burford, in the south parlor. But when he got his film developed, the picture was of another person entirely. He accused the staff of shifting the portraits, but no one had moved anything. Then, he rented a television camera and when he set up in the house to shoot film for a proposed documentary, the camera wouldn't work. When he took it back to the camera shop it worked perfectly. Was some spirit guarding the privacy of the house?

Tour guide Vickey Hoover has had a number of experiences with the "presence" in the house, although she is not in the least afraid of it. She feels it is the ghost of Benjamin Harrison. "He just has ways of letting us know he's around at times," she says. She wasn't a believer when she first joined the staff several years ago, but she soon changed her mind.

"I guess he thought I was being disrespectful and he wanted to show me," she recalls. "Anyway, I was standing in the front hall beside the linen press door when it burst open and hit me in the shoulder." This has happened to her three or four times since. "Once I was explaining the phenomenon to a group of tourists, and the door swung open again. I had to tell them I wasn't pressing any secret lever hidden under the carpet." Another time while she stood by the large piece of furniture the door opened and began swinging back and fourth. More recently, she returned after two months off on maternity leave. "One day as I stood in front of the press, I kidded with the other hostesses that Benjamin must not know I'm back. Almost as if on cue, I heard three knocks, turned, and saw the door swing open."

Both Vickey and Jennifer Hess also have heard mysterious rattles from time to time. "I was in the laundry room one day," Vickey says, "when I heard the sound. It was like a door rattling in the dining room, but no one was there. There is a candelabra in the front parlor and when anyone walks across the floor in there, you can hear the glass in it tinkling. I have heard this more than once, but each time when I checked no one was in the parlor."

Vickey also has heard a baby crying, when there was no infant in the house. "I heard it crying in the basement. I went down to look but saw nothing, and when I went back up to the breakfast room, it stopped altogether. We're really not afraid of him. He just likes to play tricks on everyone."

One day during the summer of 1984, Mrs. Jamieson called from the main house to the tour guides in an adjacent building and wanted to know who was in her attic. "We told her we didn't know of anyone," says Jan Wycoff, "but she was adamant that she heard distinct footsteps up there. She said she knew it wasn't squirrels or anything like that. It definitely was a human being's footsteps. I checked the attic and the door was bolted shut like it always is. Then I went outside to see if any workmen had any ladders against the house and were working around the attic area. I didn't see anyone."

But it is in the Berkeley dining room where most of the psychic phenomena occurs. "We don't even have to tell tourists we have a ghost," says Virginia Anders, former tour guide leader. "Many of them say they feel a presence the minute they walk into the dining room. We just smile. There is something there, but we can't explain it." Other guides nod in agreement. "I took a group into the dining room one day," says Jan Wycoff, "and the minute we entered the room a woman told me, 'you have a ghost in here. I can feel it.'"

Most of these manifestations are centered on a fruit bowl on the dining room table. Anders, for example, carefully placed a fresh apple in the bowl one morning, then before she left the room she heard it drop. She turned around and saw the apple sail through the air and go over a Chinese screen. "I got out of there real fast," she says. "I was frightened." Later, she went back. No one else had been in the room, but the apple now rested comfortably in the bowl where she had first placed it.

Such a scary experience has happened to others on the staff. Wycoff says the apples "come out on their own and fall to the floor without hitting the wide table." Once, she adds, an artificial lemon, fixed to a nail in the bowl, came out and rolled across the table on its own. Curiously, most of the fruit movements seem to occur in the winter months of January, February, and March when there are relatively few tourists afoot.

Another time Wycoff came in before the first tour one morning and found peanuts scattered across the table. "Where did they come from and how did they get there?" she asks. She told fellow guide Vickey Hoover about it, asking her to clean up the mess when she went through. Hoover saw her later and inquired, "what peanuts were you talking about. I didn't see any." They had mysteriously vanished.

"I feel the explanation of the fruit bowl in the dining room lies with Benjamin Harrison, IV," says Anders. "Maybe he didn't like the arrangement at certain times. I don't know what else to think. We know none or us do it."

The Legend of Rippon's Hollow

(Author's note: As Halloween 1998 approached, I was struck by the impressive and steadily growing number of historic houses, beds and breakfasts, and plantations which featured haunting tours. One involved three sites in Charles City County between Williamsburg and Richmond. Now, I had worked with the owners of such famous mansions as Shirley, Evelynton, and Sherwood Forest in the past, doing signings on or near October 31.

But here was a new tour, or at least new to me. Actually, it had been going on for the past four or five years, but probably was under-publicized. One of the three houses, Edgewood, was thoroughly familiar to me. I had written extensively about the alleged ghost of "Miss Lizzie," who has been seen peering out a third-story bedroom window searching for her lost lover who rode away to fight in the Civil War in the 1860s. The indefatigable owner of Edgewood, Dot Boulware, had persuaded me, on more than one occasion, to come out and sign books for her.

I knew about a second house on the tour as well. It is a B & B called North Bend. I had received one report of a scary encounter there by a guest who was so spooked she got up in the middle of the night and left the premises, vowing never to return. The third place, another B & B, was Piney Grove, and I knew virtually nothing about it. A newspaper teaser, plugging the tour, mentioned "The Legend of Rippons Hollow," would be told at Piney Grove. This looked promising, so I called Brian Gordineer one evening and asked him about it. His family owns Piney Grove.

I was at first disappointed when Brian said the legend was "kind of made up" and related by a story teller. But then he told me about a "real" ghost in the main house on the grounds, and added information about the interesting history of the plantation. Here is what he said:)

The original part of the house was built as a corn crib. It dates to 1790, and the plantation then included 300 acres. It was owned by Furneau Southall who then served as sheriff of Charles City County. Brian says in the latter part of the 19th century, and well into the 20th, a doctor and his family lived here. One of the rooms was used to operate on people. If it was a complex or complicated operation, doctors from Richmond were sent to the house to participate.

Curiously, relatively close to the original house, to which several additions have been made over the years, there is a small graveyard belonging to the doctor's family. Here, there are five grave sites for children. Halloween tour attendees are taken to this area.

Today, Piney Grove offers guests a quiet overnight stay, a history of the area, and a candlelit plantation-style breakfast. The B &

Piney Grove

B rooms are not in the main house, where Brian's parents live, but in other buildings. One is a house that was dismantled in Caroline County and reassembled on the grounds. It dates to 1857. Another was moved from a site where the Colonial Golf Course is now located. It is circa 1835. And, if one asks, Brian or one of his family will talk about their resident spirit.

The original house stood vacant and abandoned for 20 years, between 1964 and 1984. Then the Gordineers bought the property and began extensive renovations. One day, after working, Brian's father and brother were leaving when his father realized he had left his watch in the house. They went back to get it. The house was sealed tight and there was no way anyone could be inside. They had just left it.

They went inside, and both of them heard distinctive footsteps upstairs. Something was in the house. The two men searched every inch of the structure, but found nothing.

"We've not had any other experiences," Brian says. "We wonder if it was someone who might have lived here in years gone by and is there to protect the house."

There are other possible causes. Could it be the doctor who once operated at Piney Grove? One of his patients, unpleased at the outcome of his treatment? Or one of the children buried nearby? How did they die?

Perhaps it might be old Furneau Southall himself, the 18th century sheriff. For it is documented that when he died his heirs fought over ownership of the plantation for 50 years before his grandson was finally able to buy the property at auction. Would not that be enough to bring back a long-tormented spirit — to see that his house was finally in good hands?

THE RETURN OF GENERAL SHERIDAN?

(Author's note: The day after I interviewed Brian Gordineer I got a call from Ridgely Copland. She and her husband own North Bend. This impressive house — 6,000 square feet — was built in 1819, and was the home of Sarah Harrison, sister of William Henry Harrison, the ninth President of the United States, who himself was born at Berkeley, a few miles to the west. General Philip H. Sheridan used North Bend as a temporary headquarters during the Civil War, and it is said that during a temper fit in the house, he stuck his sword in one of the panel doors, splitting it.

Today, the plantation is a bed and breakfast, complete with

some historic furnishings. A solid mahogany queen tester bed, circa 1810, belonged to Edmund Ruffin, the controversial Virginia soil expert, and the man who fired the first shot at Fort Sumter to begin the Civil War. Also here is General Sheridan's desk, among illustrious other period antiques.

George Copland, incidentally, is the great-great-grandson of Ruffin, and also the great-great-nephew of William Henry Harrison. The Greek revival style home features original mantels, staircase carvings, and woodgraining on the pocket doors. There is a fireplace in each room, three porches, a billiards room, and a swimming pool. Overnight guests are treated to a lavish breakfast of bacon, sausage, homemade waffles, juice, melons and strawberries.

They may also experience a paranormal event, because both Ridgely Copland and an out-of-state guest have reported ethereal happenings, but of entirely different manifestations. Ridgely says in the past during the Halloween tours, they had an actor portray General Sheridan, but there really wasn't anything ghostly in the presentation. "We would take people through the house by candle light and then we would go up and see 'the general'," she says.

North Bend

"There was nothing out of this world, so to speak, but when we would enter the bedroom and the actor, dressed in a Civil War uniform, would get up to speak, the guests, not expecting it, would be scared to death."

Ridgely had her own encounter about ten years ago. Her husband was on a trip in Canada, and she was at North Bend alone. She was in her bedroom when she heard the sound of someone in boots tramping across the floor in the Rose Room above her. "It scared the bejammers out of me," she says. "I had never heard of anything like that before. I called my son and told him someone was in the house. He just lives a short way, and drove his truck up the lane in a matter of minutes.

"Just as I heard his truck, the stomping stopped. He searched the house from top to bottom, but found no one. He then left, and as soon as he had cleared the driveway, the heavy steps began again. I called my son back, and when he arrived, the steps ceased once more. This time he spent the night, and nothing further happened." Ridgely says this phenomenon only occurred to her that once, although a visitor also heard the footsteps one night. Ridgely wonders if the restless spirit of Philip Sheridan may still linger.

"I should add one other incident," she says. "We were doing renovations on the house in the early 1980s. An old man once came inside and asked if we had any ghosts here. I thought it was rather curious. At the time we didn't know of anything and told him so, and he reacted very strangely. He said 'don't tell me you don't have any ghosts here! I'm getting the hell out of this house,' and he left abruptly."

And there is this final note. A lady in Fairfax called the author one night and related the following:

"I don't know whether I am psychically sensitive or not. Perhaps so. I do know that my first husband died 14 years ago, and I saw him one night five years later! He was standing in the corner of a room.

"Anyway, my second husband, Richard, and I spent the night at North Bend some time ago. Mr. Copland gave us a tour of the house and then we went out to have dinner at the Indian Fields Tavern. Later, we came back and went to bed. Sometime about midnight, I noticed that Richard was still awake. I asked him what was wrong, and he told me his shoulder was bothering him.

"Shortly after that, I got the strangest feeling. I felt there was someone else in the room. I sensed there were evil spirits present. I said 'in the name of Jesus Christ, get thee behind me.' Then I clearly heard the sound of a child crying. I guessed it was someone seven or eight years old. It was a 'hurt' cry. I also saw a white wreath of live doves. And I know it was real. I wasn't dreaming.

"I bolted upright in the bed and told Richard that we had to leave here. Richard was already awake. After I told him my experience he said that he had not been able to sleep, not because of his shoulder as he had said, but because of what he was encountering in the room. He said that he had the weirdest feeling that he was 'susceptible.' Then he felt something pushing on his chest! He said it was like somebody trying to grab him. He pushed something away from him.

"Neither one of us could sleep the rest of the night. We got up at six in the morning and left. We both knew we couldn't stay there."

Oddly, one of the prized antiques at North Bend is an oriental porcelain Foo Dog dating to 1801. It is said to ward off evil spirits.

Footnote: Whether one is met by an actor or a "real" spirit at Piney Grove and North Bend, the Halloween tour has become a popular annual event. In 1998, Ridgely Copland says, more than 100 people attended.

CHAPTER 29

The 'Gray Lady' of Sherwood Forest–Part II

(Author's note: In Volume I, I wrote about the "gray lady" of Sherwood Forest, the magnificent plantation home of U.S. President John Tyler. It is located on Route 5 about 20 minutes or so west of Williamsburg. The 300-foot-long house was built around 1730, and has been in the Tyler family for more than a century and a half.

The predominant spirit here is said to be the apparitional return of a maid or servant who probably lived in the middle of the 1800s. It is believed an infant in her care died unexpectedly, and, feeling responsible, whether justified or not, the spirit returns hoping to nurse the baby back to health. The manifestations include a rocking chair that appears to rock by itself, and occasional glimpses of the wispy form of a woman dressed in gray.

Some years ago, the wife of the current owner, Payne Tyler, sat down and had a talk with the gray lady. She told her that she now lived at Sherwood Forest and that they would have to learn to "peacefully co-exist." The phenomena subsided.

When I did research for this chapter, in 1982, tour guides at the house did not mention the unearthly visitations. Since then, however, ghosts have become fashionable as tourist attractions, so when one tours here today, the legend is included during walk-throughs of the house. In fact, during Halloween week, Sherwood

Sherwood Forest

Forest and neighboring plantations sometimes host a special "haunting tour."

It was thus in October 1996, that the author was asked to revisit Sherwood Forest, to sign books for their gift shop, and to participate in an interview with Stephen Harriman, travel editor for the Virginian-Pilot, Norfolk's daily newspaper. Also participating would be Kay Tyler, Payne and Harrison Tyler's daughter-in-law.

Kay had long been a skeptic when it came to recountings of the gray lady's exploits. But, as she told Harriman, subsequent events had changed her opinion. "My husband, William, and I were staying here, and we went out to visit our cousin Alice," Kay said. "We had been talking about the gray lady. I had expressed my doubts. Alice said, 'Kay, trust me on this.' When we came back (to Sherwood) every light in the house was on. We had not left them on! And all the fireplace pokers had been knocked over. I'm sure no human being had been in here, because all the dogs were in the house."

Another time, Kay related, "We had gone to bed upstairs. It must have been 2 or 3 o'clock in the morning, something like that, when I woke up and there was this <u>feeling</u> in the room and a sort of whiteness all around. And we both distinctly heard footsteps."

Kay continued: "There was a woman here at Christmas-time, helping to serve tea. When she got ready to leave late in the afternoon, she looked out the window and saw a woman at the edge of the woods dressed in the long garb of ages ago. She called me and said, 'Kay, you're not going to believe this' . . ."

But as Harriman wrote, "Kay <u>does</u> believe now!"

Kay Tyler, Harriman and I met for the interview in the house. Of this, Harriman said, "If ever a ghost would want to make itself known, I figured it would be to Taylor. He knows of more ghosts, knows more ghost stories, than probably anybody in Virginia. We inspected the staircase and we sat listening in the Gray Room. We heard nothing. It could have been the Gray Lady's day off."

Some time later I received a letter from Mrs. Lori DiMaria of the Bronx, New York. She wrote of a strange experience she had at Sherwood Forest. Here is what she said:

"As we entered the Gray Room, I was overcome by a very strong 'presence.' This happened before our guide even mentioned the name of this room or the ghost. . . Whatever, there was an

Gray room

antique wooden chair in the corner of this room, painted black with a small flower pattern adorning it, that I could literally not take my eyes off of, and I had much trouble breathing. Whenever I tried to focus on something else in the room, I felt my eyes pulled back to this black chair like a magnet, and my eyes would start to tear! I must say it was a creepy feeling. When we were outside, Jamie said to me, 'Did you feel that chill? It was colder in there than in the rest of the house or even out here'!"

And finally there is this, from the book, "Old Williamsburg and Her Neighbors," by William Oliver Stevens, published 60 years ago: "For a good many years (after the Civil War) Sherwood Forest was tenantless, but once on a hunting trip, another John Tyler, a grandson of the President, entered the deserted house, made a fire on the hearth, and sat down before it. As the twilight of the long winter afternoon deepened, suddenly in a dark corner, an ancient music box started up and gaily played through its entire repertoire.

"This apparently had escaped destruction in 1862. Perhaps some blue-coated soldier had wound it up then, but it had indignantly refused to play for him. Then when its master, another John Tyler, entered the door, it was so happy that it played every tinkling note it possessed. At least, let us believe that is the true explanation."

The "People of the House" at Colesville

(Author's note: At the Newport News Fall Festival in October 1997, where I was autographing books, a lady came up and asked if I had ever written about Colesville Plantation. Where was it, I inquired. In Charles City County just off Route 5, she said. Are there spirits there, I asked. She nodded.)

olesville Plantation today is a 350-acre working farmland located approximately two miles west of the Charles City County courthouse and near Indian Fields Tavern, which is a charming place to dine on fine country Virginia fare. This was all part of an original 10,000-acre tract known as Swinyards and named after Thomas Swinhowe. It is also documented that the first land grant here was made in 1617, and that five years later, seven early settlers were killed on the site during the infamous Indian raid of 1622. In the mid-1700s William Cole, after whom the plantation was named, bought some of the property, and later traded this portion to three brothers named Clarke. They owned Colesville for more than 100 years before moving away in 1880.

According to family records, the noted explorers William Clark and Meriwether Lewis stayed at Colesville just prior to their departure from Charlottesville for exploration of the western territory.

Union General U.S. Grant used the house as temporary headquarters in June 1864 as he was preparing to chase Robert E. Lee and his army south, leading to the siege of Petersburg. In mid-June 1864, Grant and about 100,000 of his men crossed the James River at Wilcox Landing over a pontoon bridge near Colesville. A state historical marker notes the site where they crossed.

Little is known of the house history from 1880 well into the 20th century. In 1983, Roger and Bonnie Sizemore bought the land and house and later began renovations. Colonial Williamsburg experts helped authenticate the history of the house. It is a two story structure with original floors and trim. The earliest part of the house dates to 1730, and another part was added in 1820. Thus, it is actually two houses joined together. There are six rooms downstairs, including a kitchen, and four bedrooms upstairs plus an attic. From one bedroom one can walk up to the attic and come down in an adjacent bedroom. This secret passageway was probably built as an escape route should Indians attack. A smokehouse and an outhouse flank the main house.

Roger and Bonnie moved into Colesville in 1996. Their daughter, Arden, then was about four years old. Mysterious manifestations began the second night they were in the house. "I had heard there had been a lot of tragedy here," Bonnie says. "Several people, including some children, had died in the house. On the second night we were there, I was in the bedroom when I heard someone walking about in the bathroom. The floors here creak real bad when somebody walks on them, so there was no mistaking what I heard. Roger wasn't there. The footsteps came toward me. They entered my bedroom, walked around the bed and then went out the door and down the hall.

"I got up to look and prayed that I wouldn't see anything. I didn't. There was no one there. When Roger wasn't at home I would sometimes have Arden get in bed with me at night. We both heard the same sounds a number of times. Once it stopped right at the edge of our bed. Arden was asleep and about to fall out of the bed. I think whatever or whoever it was, was trying to alert me that she was about to fall. When I pulled Arden beside me, the footsteps left the room and went down the hall.

"I told a friend about the experiences, and she said I should talk to the ghost or ghosts. So I did. I said they were scaring me and I'd appreciate it if they wouldn't walk into my room. After that I would hear doors shut upstairs and someone walking around in the attic. But at least they weren't in my room."

Bonnie continues: "Arden had never talked to herself before, but she began doing this right after we moved in. Normally, when

Colesville

a child does this, they carry on a full conversation, but Arden didn't. It would be like she was listening to someone. She would say, 'uh huh, uh huh.' I asked her who she was talking to and she said, 'the people of the house.' She said it was a boy and a girl. Arden almost seems like she is in a trance during these conversations.

"One time Roger and Arden were in the car ready to go somewhere and Roger forgot something and left Arden in the car alone. She didn't like to be left alone and started crying. When Roger came back to the car, she told him the boy and the girl had stayed with her while he was in the house and she was okay. She described the girl as having on a long blue coat and hat, and shoes with buttons on them. The boy wore a brown hat and pants. Of course, Roger and I never saw anything, but they say sometimes a child can see spirits no one else can."

In restoring the house and attempting to get it listed on an historic register, the Sizemores called in a specialist from Chesterfield to hang some curtains. The man had never been to Colesville before and, Bonnie believes, knew nothing of its history. The moment he walked in the front door, before he even said hello, he said, "do you know you have two ghosts in this house." Bonnie was astonished. He then told her that Arden talks to the ghosts all the time, "and when she gets a little older, she will have lots of stories to tell you."

The man said that his family was sensitive to supernatural phenomena. Bonnie: "He told me that the boy ghost used to play in the attic all the time and that he used to hide stuff in a secret place in the attic, behind a loose brick. Roger went up to investigate, and he found the loose brick and an open space behind it! The man then said that I shouldn't be afraid of the spirits, that they wouldn't harm me. They were just looking after the house. He said that there was a strong box somewhere on the property. I felt a chill up my spine when he said this, because I had been having recurrent dreams about such a strong box. He said I should find it. We haven't found it yet, but Roger is into metal detection and we have found all sorts of Civil War relics.

"We also had some contractors during the renovation who said strange things happened to them. They said someone or something would turn lights on and off, and that their tools and materials would get 'moved around' when they weren't there."

Roger and Bonnie have opened a bed and breakfast at Colesville. Their scrumptious breakfasts include pear jams and dried apples from the trees on the farm. Wheat, barley and corn are grown on the plantation. Whether or not visitors will sense the spirits of a boy and girl, as the Sizemores have, is not known.

Who are these children of the past? Bonnie has a clue. The amateur psychic who came in to hang the curtains, said the girl's name was Emily and the boy's name was Trent. Bonnie did some research. She wrote to a Clarke family descendent in Alabama. He told her the last Clarke to live in the house was named Alexander Trent Clarke!

"The curtain hanger told me that the boy and girl have remained here because they felt this was still their house, says Bonnie. "They would be friendly to us because we had faithfully restored Colesville. But to be on the safe side, we have hung a picture of Mr. Clarke in one of the rooms. We hope he likes that."

The Ghostly Reenactment of Jeb Stuart's Ride

He was charismatic, flamboyant, dashing, daring, debonair the living embodiment of Southern pride and spirit. If Robert E. Lee exemplified the dignity and integrity of "The Cause," he typified the flair and savoir faire.

He dressed for the part. His uniform included a gold-braided jacket with a yellow sash and a re-lined cavalry cape, knee-high jack boots, and a felt hat with pinned up brim and ostrich-feather plume. He wanted to be, and, in fact, was known to be the last cavalier. He was the Sir Lancelot of the Civil War.

His exploits were of the nature of which legends are made. For three years, he dashed and slashed his way in and out of enemy lines, causing both embarrassment and dread. He himself was without fear. He was brave, courageous, and outrageously defiant. He veritably thumbed his nose at his adversaries and challenged them to catch him if they were good enough. They couldn't. In a war full of gigantic heroes, he stood among the tallest.

There was never a dull moment under his command. He was revered by his men and loved by Southerners with an adulation on a level with that accorded only to two other men—Robert E. Lee and Stonewall Jackson.

Confederate General W. B. Taliaferro may have put it best when he said, "He was the best cavalryman America ever produced."

This was James Ewell Brown Stuart!

Though he was only 31-years-old when a Union sharpshooter's

bullet struck him down, his exploits during the war have filled books. And the colorful anecdotes attributed to Jeb Stuart have made such volumes a course of excitement and entertainment for more than a century and a quarter.

Jeb Stuart was mortally wounded at the Battle of Yellow Tavern near Ashland, north of Richmond on May 11, 1864.

The general was brought to the home of his brother-in-law, Dr. Charles Brewer, on West Grace Street, where he was visited by Confederate President Jefferson Davis. One of his last requests was for the group surrounding him to sing his favorite hymn, "Rock of Ages." Consoled with the thought of being reunited with his daughter, Flora, who had died in 1862, he passed away at 7:30 p.m. on May 12,1864.

He was buried the next day in Hollywood Cemetery. The funeral was attended by President Davis and hundreds of local residents. It was said that "not since the death of Stonewall Jackson in 1863 had the South felt such a blow."

Does Stuart's ghost — and the apparitional spirits of his cavalrymen — occasionally return to relive some of his legendary charges? Possibly. There is at least one recorded account of his spectral return at the site of perhaps his most famous feat of all.

It was June 1862. Union General George McClellan, with an army of more than 100,000 men and an enormous arsenal of weapons and supplies, was plodding westward across Charles City County bordering the James River, toward Richmond. General Lee was deeply concerned about the size, strength, and strategy of McClellan's command. He was considering a strong frontal attack. He called on Stuart to lead a reconnaissance mission to gather such vital information. Lee deemed it necessary for Stuart only to go far enough to assess the situation, and then report back of him.

But the dashing cavalier saw in this probing operation an opportunity to again humiliate his opponents. Instead of parrying, thrusting and then retreating, he decided not only to reach the enemy lines, but to ride completely around them!

From a point north of Richmond, Stuart assembled 1,200 of his best horsemen and began his movement at 2 a.m. on June 12, 1862. He told no one of their mission or destination. As they moved eastward on the second day, Stuart's men encountered some resistance from a Yankee picket post shortly after crossing the Totopotomoy Creek.

Here, Captain William Latané of the 9th Virginia led a charge

Jeb Stuart

directly into the enemy. With a slash of his saber, he wounded a Union officer, but he was then killed by two pistol shots. He was the only man to die during this extraordinary ride.

After routing the remaining forces, Stuart's men moved on. By the time they reached a place called Old Church, Stuart had gathered all the data he needed to brief Lee. But instead of turning homeward, he then, characteristically, chose to keep moving east, sweeping around behind McClellan's forces, and then going south to the James River and north back to Richmond, past the entire army; a once-in-a-lifetime chance to thrust the ultimate defiant taunt at the Yankees.

It was Friday the 13th. Jeb Stuart viewed it as his destiny.

He pressed forward. By now, the Federals knew he was in their midst, and they sent forces after him. The Confederates destroyed supplies, burned a 75-wagon supply train, and took prisoners as they went. On the morning of June 14, they reached the Chickahominy River.

Here, they faced a problem. The river was swollen and running high and fast from heavy storms over the past several weeks. It was too dangerous to be forded. The Forge Bridge had been destroyed a month earlier when General Joseph Johnston's men had retreated through the area. Union forces were now in full pursuit. Ever resourceful, Stuart ordered a makeshift bridge to be built, using timbers from a nearby barn.

It was during the construction of this bridge that Jeb Stuart may have lain down on the banks of the river, to repose. He and his men had had little rest and practically no sleep since they had begun their journey.

The long column of men crossed the bridge and then set it afire. Their timing couldn't have been better. As the bridge was burning, the first Federal forces reached the Chickahominy. All they could do was look on in chagrined admiration as the last of the Rebels waved at them from the other side.

Stuart then, unthreatened, rode 35 miles west back to Richmond and reported to Lee. When his men followed, intact except for Captain Latané, they received a rousing hero's welcome.

A century later, to the day, June 13, 1962, two Virginia couples picnicked at the site of Stuart's historic crossing of the Chickahominy. One of the men was named Edmund Farley. The other man was Bill Latané, the great, great grand nephew of Captain William Latané! What happened to them on that warm spring day was recorded by the noted author, Nancy Roberts, in her book on Civil War ghosts.

Farley, Roberts wrote, wandered off from the others and walked along the banks of the river searching for a clue as to where the old Forge Bridge may have stood. After a while he lay down to take a nap. When he awoke, a strange thing happened. He heard men's voices and the sounds of "pounding hammers and the sharp crack of planks striking one another." But he could see nothing. It was, he felt, as if an invisible team were building a bridge!

Farley then noticed "a bearded sleeping figure lying on the

ground near him." The figure was dressed in the uniform of a Confederate officer, complete with a bright yellow sash. Beside him was a black felt hat with a long plume tucked under its band, and a beautiful sword. Farley wondered if the man was dead. Then he saw that the figure was breathing. He reached down and touched the figure. Its blue eyes opened, and it spoke. "It's all right. Get some rest." The figure then smiled. "Don't worry," it said, "my cavalry will get the bridge built in time, and, if not, we will all have plenty of excitement when the Yankees catch up with us."

It was already enough excitement for Farley. He was dumbfounded, speechless. For a fleeting moment he wondered if he had somehow stumbled into some sort of historic time warp . . . the sounds of hammering, the voices of the men . . . the figure of the Confederate officer lying on the ground. How does one explain this? As he walked back to the picnic area, his only rational explanation was that a reenactment of some kind was going on, and the figure was an actor in it, who had stopped, as he had, to rest. It had to be. There could be no other answer. Or could there be? Meanwhile, Bill Latané and the two ladies had encountered another phenomenon. As they neared the road which led back to the highway, they saw an entire troop of mounted Confederate soldiers led by a cavalry officer. The officer was wearing the same uniform the figure wore that Farley had seen; thigh-length black leather boots, yellow sash, and a hat with a brilliant feather!

Noise broke the spell. Latané looked up and saw a convoy of modern military vehicles on the road. When he looked back towards the site of the "reenactment," the Civil War soldiers had vanished!

Edmund Farley, who had seen the vision of the Confederate officer that same day, checked with authorities about the reenactment. He was told that one had been planned, but it had, at the last moment, been canceled because a military convoy was to move through the area!

CHAPTER 32

The Confederate War Soldier Who Died <u>Twice!</u>

(Author's note: Strange is not a strong enough word to explain how I sometimes gather ghostly material in Virginia. Consider this: In my book, "Civil War Ghosts of Virginia," (1995), I wrote, in the introduction, how I was surprised that some of the most tragic and traumatic battle sites of that war seemed not to be haunted. One of these places is Malvern Hill, located between Richmond and Williamsburg just off historic Route 5 in Charles City County.

As a preface to the following extraordinary account, let me repeat what I said: "Why are there no spirits, or at least more evidence of spirits at Malvern Hill? It was here, on July 1, 1862, that thousands of Confederates charged up a long, gently-sloping hill in the face of murderous cannon and rifle fire. Many were killed. The dreadful carnage was described by Union Colonel William W. Averell, who, as the foggy dawn broke the next morning, wrote: 'Our ears had been filled with agonizing cries from thousands before the fog was lifted, but now our eyes saw an appalling spectacle upon the slopes down to the woodlands half a mile away.

"'Over 5,000 dead and wounded men were on the ground in every attitude of distress. A third of them were dead or dying, but enough were alive and moving to give the field a singular crawling effect.' Yet despite the agony of such a disaster, there have been only a couple of vague reports of witnesses who, more than a century later, told of hearing strange noises and moans across the fields, and of catching fleeting glimpses of distant disembodied figures at Malvern Hill where blood once dyed the ground red."

hat is what I wrote in 1995. I have since learned, through Nannette Morrison's fine book, "Echoes of Valor," that there have indeed been a few instances of unexplained ethereal encounters at Malvern Hill. With Ms. Morrison's gracious permission, I quote: "There are two women from the Sandston area of Richmond who are quite drawn to the Malvern Hill Battlefield. The pair always bring their dogs to let them run, but the real affinity for the acreage goes beyond that. 'Every time I come out here, I get a real eerie feeling. Still, something keeps drawing us to this wheatfield.' The older woman points to the wood line on the left, 'See that spot out there? One afternoon last year I swear I saw two Confederate boys running along that edge, coming toward us!' She was adamant regarding the sighting.

"A few folks who live around the Malvern Hill site have also remarked on seeing and hearing unusual phenomena. Tim Fredrikson was a house guest of some friends living only two miles from the battlefield. One July evening in 1994, Tim was driving his car about dark and drawing near the residence. Through a patch of woods on Route 156 approaching Malvern Hill, an event startled him. A caisson and limber were drawn across the road

Malvern Hill

directly in front of his vehicle about 150 yards away! They passed from one wooded side to the other as quick as a flash! Yet, for Tim there was no denying what he witnessed."

Ms. Morrison then described the battle scene, recreating the awful sounds that emanated that fateful day — the chorus of Rebel yells as the infantry charged up the hill amidst the booming roar of General George McClellan's imposing line of cannon. Then she told of another haunting account experienced by a park volunteer named Martin. "Was it these same sounds that Martin heard in July 1993? He is certain that it is true. Martin was alone at his post in early July . . . when he was interrupted by voices. 'I looked around to see who was approaching (he said), but there was no one around. . . The fields are wide open. There weren't any cars in sight either. I sat quietly in the shade of the park shelter right where the cannon are now. Then I heard them again. I distinctly heard two men carrying on a regular conversation. I couldn't quite determine complete sentences. Nevertheless, there was a clear exchange of words back and forth only a few feet from me.' (Martin then checked two of the houses that are adjacent to the battlefield and found no one home, and thus no rational explanation for what he was hearing. He returned to the shelter.) He then said, 'This was really puzzling! Anyway, I stayed at my post for the afternoon. Every once in a while I could catch bits of that same conversation back in time once again. And actually, there were many days I spent there that I felt some real creepy things, almost like eyes watching me from all sides'."

In 1997, reenactors of the 12th Virginia Infantry gathered at Malvern Hill to take part in a living history recreation of the battle which had taken place 135 years earlier. For her most recent book, "Warrior Poets and Warrior Saints," (Echo Effects Publishing, Charlottesville, $15.95) Nannette Morrison later interviewed several members of the group when it was learned that strong psychic activity had taken place on the battlefield the night before the anniversary of the battle.

Reenactor sergeant Henry Kidd told author Morrison that the 12th Virginia unit had been portraying camp life that night, and during the evening one young man went from campsite to campsite reading a letter which a Georgia soldier had written to his mother on the eve of the battle in 1862. According to Kidd and others, the reenactor's portrayal was so lifelike that some reported getting chills, and one swore that he saw the images of 15 or so real Confederate soldiers standing nearby during the readings!

At this point Tim Fredrikson, the same person Nannette Morrison had quoted in her earlier book, said that he was "being drawn" toward the tree line flanking the battlefield, about 200 yards away. Several of the men started walking toward the woods, and when they got near they felt a sharp drop in the temperature. They had walked into a cold spot. Such spots are often associated with the presence of spirits. Sergeant Kidd then stepped backwards a few feet and the temperature returned to normal. When he advanced again he was once more enveloped in coldness.

Nearer the treeline, which seemed to be drawing the reenactors closer to it, Kidd said he suddenly smelled the strong presence of body odor. He looked around. There was no one near him. The odor seemed to be hanging in one particular spot, and then, in a few seconds, it dissipated.

Then Kidd had a sighting. Morrison quoted him: "In the treeline under the limbs of the trees where it is dark and the tree trunks are, and between that area and where the brushline starts, is a real dark area. That is the space where I saw silhouetted shapes of men's heads, shoulders and elbows bent back to their sides as though they were holding muskets centered in front of them. It wasn't one or two, but an entire regiment of Confederate soldiers from 135 years ago standing there in front of me! Moving toward the regiment was like observing an Impressionistic painting. As I moved closer to them, I could no longer make out individual forms. If I stepped back, I could again see details. Yet, the entire area was illuminated with an unusual shadowy light. . . I stood near the Confederate ranks and had the sensation of the soldiers closing in around me. 'Thanks!' was the clear message I felt from them."

According to Morrison, a most extraordinary psychic phenomenon also occurred during that evening. Those who witnessed it said that the voice of a 17-year-old Confederate soldier spoke through the body of reenactor Tim Fredrikson! Henry Kidd was one of those who heard this. He said the soldier identified himself as Samuel Edmunds of Tazewell, Virginia (Subsequent research of Civil War Records determined that a Samuel Edmunds of the 26th Virginia Infantry was, in fact, at Malvern Hill for the battle. It was not known whether or not he survived.)

The "voice" let it be known that he was frightened. He was afraid of being killed the next day in battle. He also expressed concern that if he was killed, would he be admitted into heaven? Sergeant Kidd and others tried to console the shaken youth, and prayed with him. They believe it helped.

There was yet another encounter that night. Reenactor Whitt Smith and his son Christian also felt compelled to approach the mysterious woods. Sergeant Kidd followed them and told Morrison: "As we arrived at the slight rise where you could barely see the treeline, the ghostly unit was still visible and waiting. As he (Whitt) slowly stepped into the midst of them, the Confederate regiment parted ranks as if to admit a fellow soldier . . . the color party for the regiment closed ranks around him, accepting him as a member."

That is what Nannette Morrison wrote. Here, let me add a personal note; one that is shared by a number of historians. Both commanding generals at this site — Robert E. Lee and George McClellan — made monumental blunders at Malvern Hill. Lee's mistake was to overestimate the abilities of his men in ordering them to charge up that fearful hill in the face of such overpowering cannon and rifle fire. It was an order, against all odds, that Lee was to repeat by directing Pickett's charge at Gettysburg a year later. There was simply no way a run up Malvern Hill against such awesome force was going to be successful.

McClellan, on the other hand, did not follow up his advantage. With Lee's men in total disarray, he should have ordered them to march on toward Richmond, barely 20 miles away. Yet, incredibly, despite the severe damage he had caused, he chose instead to retreat and regroup. Had he gone forward, many experts believe, he could have taken Richmond with his far superior forces and possibly shortened the war by two or three years. It was his extreme cautiousness that eventually led to his removal as commanding general of the Union forces.

And now, to one of the most surrealistic encounters I have come across in nearly two decades of researching ghost experiences in the commonwealth. I was at a New Age festival held in Williamsburg in September 1998, giving a talk. In the question and answer session afterwards a young lady raised her hand and asked if I had ever interviewed anyone who had their body invaded by a spirit from the past. I told her of the lady in Charlottesville, who, while living in an old house near Monticello, believed that the spirit of a former slave, circa 1820s, had taken over her body for a few minutes. (See "The Ghosts of Virginia, Volume I," 1993.) The woman said she felt she was that slave; she felt the slave's tiredness from having too many children and from having been worked too hard. The feeling passed in about three or four minutes.

Here then is what the lady, Beth Wells of Richmond, told me about her experiences at Malvern Hill: "It was in June 1998, near the anniversary of the battle. I was in my car, alone, and driving on Willis Church Road. It was mid-afternoon and it was a beautiful day. I remember saying to myself how gorgeous the woods looked, when, at that very instance, I felt the presence of a spirit in the car with me. It suddenly was there, in my body! It was the presence of a young Confederate soldier, and he, or it, said 'That's the last thing I thought,' meaning he, too, had noticed how beautiful the woods were.

"And then, I felt — I knew — that he had just been shot. He had been shot in the solar plexus. The shot tore a hole in his chest. He lifted his hands up in the air, and in that instant he was gone. The presence had left the car. It was like he had taken up residence in my body for a few fleeting seconds. I don't know how else to describe it.

"It was like he had been trying to communicate with me, like he wanted me to know he had been killed. The strangest thing was that it wasn't at all a frightening experience. It was, rather, a shar-

ing kind of thing. He wanted me to know about him. I felt privileged.

"I know it all may sound crazy, but it really happened. I was fully awake and lucid. I guess the sensation lasted only a few seconds, but it was very real. It did happen! I have tried to come up with an explanation. Did I somehow drive through his energy field for those few seconds. I don't know.

"I will say this, however. I feel much less afraid of death now."

A FAMILY BURIAL

There is a fascinating footnote to the battle at Malvern Hill. It was recorded by author Nannette Morrison in her 1998 book, "Warrior Poets and Warrior Saints." Her research uncovered a singular incident that most absorbingly reveals the harsh ironies of war. During the fighting a Union sergeant named Driscoll shot a Confederate officer. He later went to see if the man was dead. As the sergeant turned him over the young man said, "Father?" He then closed his eyes. He was dead. Driscoll had killed his own son, who had moved to the south before the Civil War started! Minutes later the sergeant's unit was ordered to charge. He was mortally wounded. Both father and son were buried in a single grave on the battlefield, marked only with a rough cross.

CHAPTER 3 3

Skull & Crossbones

Odds and Ends of the Curious and Unexplained

A Will Most Strange

he following will is extracted and excerpted from Williamsburg's Virginia Gazette, May 28, 1767. The author of the will obviously had some strong opinions, particularly about lawyers, the clergy, and women.

"_____, being sound both in mind and body do therefore think this the best and properest time of making my last will and testament, for as I have no great opinion of man's understanding being present at a time that his body is weak and indisposed, I find myself under an obligation of swearing at this conjecture from the usage of mankind, of declaring my will at a season in which I find both body and mind influenced by the utmost vigor and sanity.

"I leave my body as a very wholesome feast to the worms inhabiting the vault of my family to whom I acknowledge myself extremely indebted for eating up my ancestors; particularly for their kindness in demolishing an old tesky (sic) father, who left to me at his death 50,000 pounds, although he was near about starving me during his life.

"To all practicing solicitors and attorneys I bequeath the following proverb, viz. 'Honesty is the best policy.' And this legacy I chose to give to those worthy gentlemen, it being the only one I can

think of for which I can be sure they would not quarrel.

"To all unmarried women I bequeath cleanliness.

"To all coquettes I leave her a rotten reputation and the contempt of every man of sense.

"To all prudes, from my soul I bequeath virginity and wrinkles; or if they prefer having a bastard by their father's butler, groom or coachman, or any other butler, groom, etc., I desire my executors to give them their choice.

"To the Parson of my Parish and all other Parsons, I leave the following piece of advice: that they would not any longer expose their own weakness and absurdity by attempting to explain things which are mysteries, and consequently incomprehensible and above all explanation, and that instead of tiring their congregations with what they call demonstrations, they would be pleased to enforce the practice of that reviving system of morality which our Lord Jesus Christ came down from Heaven to deliver to mankind.

"To my three brothers, I leave my whole estate real and personal; to be divided equally among them; share and share alike, and my will is that if ever they marry, they should settle one farthing penny pin money to their wives. . ."

From a Disenchanted Husband

Here's a poem published in the Virginia Gazette, March 16, 1738, obviously from another woman hater:
"Of all the Plaques beneath the Sun,
To love's the greatest Curse;
If one's deny'd then he's undone;
If not, 'tis ten times worse.
Lovers the Strangest Fools are made,
When they their Nymphs pursue;
Which they will ne'er believe 'til Wed,
But then they find it true.
They beg, they pray, and they implore,
Til wearied out of Life;
And pray what's all this trouble for?
Why truly for a Wife.
Each Maid's an Angel while she's woo'd,
But when the Wooing's done,
The Wife, instead of Flesh and Blood,
Proves nothing but a Bone."

The Curse of the Cats

The following is excerpted from the October 1974 issue of "Williamsburg Today:"
"The hearthside cat takes on a new form at Halloween, becoming the Devil's disciple and the Witch's companion. A black cat, especially, is suspected of supernatural powers, of being Lucifer's messenger and a harbinger of evil.
"Because cats had been deified in Egypt and consecrated by the Greeks, they were symbols of paganism to the early Christians.

Chiswell-Bucktrout House

But a modern authority on witchcraft believes that 'the cat's predominance in folk memory has less to do with ancient pagan belief than it had with the simple fact that old women — who were the most likely to be suspected of witchcraft — kept cats.'

"However, The Devil's Bible stated bluntly: 'Only imbeciles do not know that all cats have a pact with the Devil'."

The Ghost Made Up for Television

Is there a ghost at the Chiswell-Bucktrout house? According to some Colonial Williamsburg employees, guests have reported some strange incidents there.

They have told of glasses moving, clothes falling from hangers, mysterious footsteps, and unexplained voices in the hallway at night.

Could it be the one-time owner of the house Colonel John Chiswell? He has been described as a "testy and choleric man with a fierce temper."

During a drunken brawl in 1766, Chiswell ran a sword through his "friend," Robert Routledge, and killed him. He was charged with murder.

Before his trial came up, however, he died. And to this day, there seems to be some confusion as to how he expired. His physician said he died from "nervous fits" owing to constant uneasiness of mind. Others, though, speculate he took his own life.

In either case, when his body was prepared for burial, a bizarre incident occurred. Routledge's friends followed the coffin and demanded that it be opened to verify that the corpse was that of Chiswell. It was.

Thus one might think that if there is a ghost at the Chiswell-Bucktrout house, it might well be the colonel himself. But then, why would his spirit appear in Williamsburg and not at the site where he died, near Richmond? Such questions, of course, have no answers.

And so, in October 1995, a film crew from the network television show, Good Morning America, came to town in search of a haunted house. They stayed at the Chiswell-Bucktrout house. They were there to film an episode for a Halloween airing.

They wanted to create a reenactment of Colonel Chiswell in ghostly form. The problem was no one knew what he looked like! There are no known likenesses of him.

So they videotaped an actor in colonial costume walking through the Raleigh Tavern, and, with special effects, he appeared as an apparition.

If Colonel Chiswell has not appeared as a ghost either at his grave site, his house in Williamsburg, or at the Raleigh Tavern, he certainly would have just cause to materialize now, if only to set the record straight.

Cause for a Ghostly Return?

In December 1978, a frail, footless skeleton washed up in a marshy area near Yorktown Beach. The arms were crossed over the chest. After examination by the state medical examiner's office in Richmond, it was determined that the remains were those of a Revolutionary War soldier, "probably buried in a cemetery that had been engulfed by the York River."

In a newspaper article covering the event was this odd note: "The discovery of such skeletons is not uncommon in this historic part of Tidewater, according to the park rangers. Nothing is done with the remains that float up; instead, it is left to the wind and tides to carry them back out into the river. Researchers know where the underwater burial grounds are located and can conduct archeological digs if they desire."

Where Are My Witch Doors?

In the early days of Williamsburg it was not uncommon to find "witch doors" in old houses. These doors featured a cross on them, with the bottom part of the cross representing an open Bible.

Such doors were superstitiously believed to keep any witch or evil spirit out of whatever room the door closed on. Although they have not been known as witch doors for generations, a few can still be found in and around Williamsburg.

The 'Snapdragon Lady'

One of the more eccentric personalities of 19th century Williamsburg was a woman named Charlotte Bingham Davis, who told everyone who would listen that she was the great-granddaughter of an English princess once married to a Danish king. While details of that royal union are sketchy, there is a tradition that the king treated his wife cruelly, and to escape she was smuggled out of the country in a coffin, eventually winding up as a lady's maid in Virginia.

Whatever, in her later years in life, Mrs. Davis, impoverished, depended upon the support of the church and friends for her sustenance. Even so, many feared giving her food, due to what was described as a "most fiery temper." If, for example, her soup bowl was not filled to the brim she would heartily chastise the unlucky person who had brought it to her. In fact, her tirades became so legendary that few dared darken her doorstep.

When she died she was laid to rest in the Bruton Parish cemetery. The markings on her grave have been washed away in time, but there may be a way to tell where she lies. Although her ghost has not returned to chide her neighbors, it was said by those who knew her then, that the only flowers that would flourish on her tombstone . . . were snapdragons!

A Witness from the Beyond

In "Legends of Virginia Courthouses," published by the Dietz Printing Company in 1933, author John H. Gwathmey recounts a humorous event involving attorney C. A. Branch of Williamsburg, and his "star witness," a black man named Elijah White. It was the early 1900s, and it seems the two men's paths crossed a number of times, mostly when Branch was defending White from a variety of different charges ranging from disorderly conduct to assault to "intent to mayhem."

Some said it was not so much Branch's lawyering, but more the guile and shrewdness of White that allowed the defendant to invariably escape conviction, even though, as author Gwathmey noted, "he was constantly getting into trouble of one kind or another." In fact, White was acquitted so many times one judge remarked there was no use arresting him anymore. He was so cunning that Branch not infrequently called upon White as a witness in other trials.

Some years later Branch passed away, and "not very long afterward," Elijah White was struck and killed by a railroad train. Within a day or two a citizen of Williamsburg stopped by one day at Captain Bob Timberlake's store and passed on the news. Captain Bob had known both Branch and White well and had been either a witness or a juror at some of White's trials.

When he was told of White's accident, he proclaimed: "Fo Gawd, Mr. Branch has got in trouble and sent for his witness!"

The Perils of Drink

This from the February 19, 1773, issue of the Virginia Gazette in Williamsburg: "Departed this life, in the 50th year of his age, Thomas Low Thimble, after a series of bouts of drunkenness. It may be with truth be said, that no man ever died less regretted; the sound of his last trumpet gave a general joy to all his friends, as well as those who had the misfortune to be of his acquaintance. Take heed, ye sons of Bacchus, that when Death comes with his summons you may not be caught napping; as you see, was the case with Mr. Thimble!"

More Baffling Revelations at Bacon's Castle

(Author's note: No ferry ride across the James River from Jamestown to Surry County would be complete without a visit to historic Bacon's Castle. I covered the multiple psychic events which have occurred there over the centuries in Volume I of "The Ghosts of Williamsburg." There have been, for instance:

— A red velvet rocking chair that rocks by itself.

— The late-night sounds of descending footsteps, and of unexplained "horrible moaning."

— Glass globes shattered and large dictionaries flung across rooms by unseen hands.

— The "pulsating, red ball of fire" sometimes seen rising from the nearby graveyard at Old Lawne's Creek Church. It is said to soar 30 to 40 feet in the air, float or hover above castle grounds, and then disappear from sight.

Since the initial publication of that chapter in 1983, there have been more reports of psychic happenings in Bacon's Castle, which was built "sometime after 1655." The building, incidentally, is named for Nathaniel Bacon, of "Bacon's Rebellion" fame. In 1676, a number of his followers stayed here.)

I t is interesting to note a couple of romantic incidents which occurred at the castle. There is one window where Emmet Robinson had the following poem to his wife etched: "In storm or sunshine - joy and strife, thou art my

Bacon's Castle

own, my much loved wife, treasure blessings of my life."

There is the Civil War romance of Virginia Hankins, whose father owned the house at the time, and the dashing young Confederate soldier, Sidney Lanier, who later was to become one of the South's most famous and most eloquent poets. Stationed nearby, Lanier was a frequent visitor in 1863 and 1864, and became entranced with the lovely and well educated "'Ginna." He wrote to friends that they had become "soul-friends," and that, as he read the works of great poets to her, "she is in a perfect blaze of enthusiasm."

Often during this idyllic interlude from the horrible war being waged around them, Ginna and Sidney would ride off into the green woods of Surry County, picnic, talk and plan. Lanier affectionately called her his "Little Brown Bird." And when, in August 1864, he was called away with his unit he pledged to return as soon as possible so they could be married.

They wrote to each other frequently but when Mrs. Hankins

died, Ginna felt her first responsibility was to care for her grief-stricken father and his seven young sons. Sadly, she rejected Lanier's proposal. Still, although he eventually married, and created the works which are revered to this day, they corresponded faithfully for the rest of their lives in the form of poetry.

Historical interpreters at Bacon's Castle say that paranormal activities continue to this day. "From time to time, we get visitors who feel very uncomfortable here," one guide said. "They almost immediately sense some sort of supernatural presence when they walk in the door."

Richard Rennolds, curator of the castle from 1973 to 1981, used to tell of the time one morning at 3:30 when he was awakened by the sound of his two-and-a-half year old son laughing in his crib in an upstairs bedroom. "Daddy, where's the lady?" The child asked Rennolds when he reached him. "What lady?" Rennolds said. "The lady with the white hands. She was tickling me."

On another occasion, a few years later, a tour guide was standing in the great hall one morning before the castle was opened to the public when "something" ran by her from the outside passageway and went through the hall and into another chamber on the other side. She heard feet running on the hardwood floor but did not see anyone. As the sound of the steps were passing by, something brushed her arm and gave her a chill.

The same hostess also said there had been strange noises a number of times, most commonly loud popping and crackling sounds, which sometimes were heard by people in the video reception room. They were too much for one young couple who heard the noise and became so frightened they left the castle even before the tour started.

There are many theories as to just why Bacon's Castle may be haunted. Some say Nathaniel Bacon's lieutenants, many of whom were executed by Governor Berkeley in 1676, may linger here, the site of their last hideout. There is a contention that the spirit of Ginna Hankins, Sidney Lanier's love during the Civil War, returns to lament "what might have been." Area oldtimers, however, point to the brilliant comet that flashed across the skies here more than 300 years ago, and say it was a forewarning that much tragedy and bloodshed would follow in its wake.

But does anyone really know?

CHAPTER 35

Something That
'Swooshed' at Chippokes

o they or don't they . . . have any ghosts at the old mansion at Chippokes State Park, on the south side of the James River about halfway between the towns of Smithfield on the east, and Surry on the west?

Maybe they do, maybe they don't. It depends on who you speak to. The park manager and chief ranger decline to talk about any unusual psychic activity there, but other employees and visitors say some strange things have happened to them while on the grounds.

Either way, Chippokes — the park and the house — are both scenic and historic, and well worth a tour. Just down the road from the more famous (and more haunted) Bacon's Castle, the property here was first occupied in 1612. By 1616, a land grant had been given to Captain William Powell, and he chose the name "Choupocke," a friendly Indian chief in the area at that time. Ironically, Powell was killed in the great Indian massacre of 1622. (Whether or not Choupocke was one of those who became unfriendly is not known.)

Chippokes has been a working farm for more than 350 years. Corn, grain, tobacco and apples were the main crops in the 17th and 18th centuries; peanuts and tobacco in the 19th century; and a variety of crops as well as livestock in the 20th.

The mansion itself was built about 1854 in the plain Greek revival style. Several early outbuildings and farm structures, stretched along a lane, preserve the plantation atmosphere. According to "The Virginia Guide," written more than 50 years ago, the main house "was built to conform with the early pattern that involved a river view, beaded weatherboarding and chimneys and dormers. On the grounds are slave houses that bear testimony, in their comfortable and well-designed simplicity, to the 'ante-bellum' prosperity of the plantation."

Another author has written that Chippokes "commands a magnificent panoramic view of the lower James . . . and radiates the charming atmosphere of years of long ago . . . But the highlight of the estate is the five-mile drive over fertile fields, through shadowy woods, down to the sandy beach at the river's edge."

Such a view is enjoyed by thousands of visitors each year, and every July an annual "Pork, Peanut and Pine" festival is held here, including live entertainment (country and gospel music), craft demonstrations, and mouth-watering barbecue and peanut pies.

Chippokes was given to the commonwealth in 1967 by Mrs. Victor Stewart "to serve as a learning center for the history of Virginia agriculture." She and her husband had purchased the estate in 1917. Some believe it may be Mrs. Stewart who has made her presence known at Chippokes long after she had departed this earth.

One who does is Jo-An Miller, a volunteer tour guide at the park. She was in the mansion on a rainy day in 1997 when there were no tourists around. She got out some sewing. All of a sudden the front door sprang open by itself, a coldness enveloped the room, and "something" swooshed by her, "whirling like a dervish." "I saw only hair and fabric," she recalls, "but not the face or real form of a human being." It swished by her toward the double glass doors inside the hallway and then went <u>through</u> the unopened doors.

Jo-An thinks it may well have been the spirit of Mrs. Stewart. "They had been doing extensive renovations to the house, and maybe she didn't like what they were doing," she says. Chief ranger and curator Catherine Correll says a number of tourists have reported strange sounds and sightings in the house and on the grounds, but she is reluctant to pass them on.

A receptionist at Chippokes did say that a local young lady had a rather frightening experience a few years ago. She had come to the mansion after it had closed for the day, and was sitting on the front steps when she heard footsteps behind coming down toward her. She assumed it was a park employee. As the steps neared her she looked around. There was no one there. She ran to her car as fast as she could and drove away.

So there may well be spirits about at Chippokes, even if the officials there don't want to talk about them.

CHAPTER 36

Unaccountable Events at Upper Brandon

(Author's note: I am indebted to the respected Virginia artist, Parks Pegram Duffie, III, for leading me to this chapter. While interviewing Parks regarding his haunted house in Petersburg, he told me about some extraordinary phenomena at historic Upper Brandon Plantation, on the James River in Prince George County, south of the city of Hopewell.

"I once did a commission painting for the owners there," Parks said, "and they showed me some really wild photos. They were taken of two little girls in front of a fireplace in the house. It appears that something from the fire seems to swirl around and envelop the girls. I know the former owner of Upper Brandon. Would you like me to call her?" Indeed. Subsequent calls and visits led to a most interesting account.)

pper Brandon has a charm all its own. It was constructed in the early part of the 19th century by William Byrd Harrison, son of Benjamin Harrison of Brandon, and the former Evelyn Taylor Byrd of Westover. She incidentally, was a niece of Miss Evelyn Byrd of Westover, who is said to haunt that plantation.

Upper Brandon, a short distance west of Brandon is situated on a gradual slope lying close to the James River, and is heavily timbered in willow oaks, ash and magnolia. The oaks, one writer described, "have made a prodigious growth in this congenial soil and cannot fail to interest the lover of old trees."

Mr. Harrison was known as one of the most progressive planters of his time, and is acknowledged as being a pioneer (along with Edmund Ruffin) in the use of lime for coastal lands. He is credited with bringing the estate back to a high state of fertility after it had been exhausted by years of intensive farming in grain and tobacco.

The general plan of the house is much like the older Brandon, though the lines are more massive and the wings are smaller. Terraced boxwood and serpentine pathways lead from the front of the mansion to the river's edge. The old garden, however, suffered greatly from 1862 to 1865, during the Civil War, and was never completely restored.

In fact, the residence was occupied by Federal soldiers who, as one writer put it, "as usual, left their sabre gashes on the balustrades and bullet holes in the paneled walls. One of the owner's sons at the time, Benjamin Harrison, was killed in battle at nearby Malvern Hill while fighting for the South.

Today, Upper Brandon is owned by the James River Corporation, a large company headquartered in Richmond. The house and grounds are used as an executive "retreat." The corpora-

Upper Brandon

tion has done a marvelous job of maintenance and restoration.

"There are a lot of ghost stories associated with Upper Brandon," says Mrs. Elizabeth Dehan of Cincinnati, Ohio. She is related to a former owner of the mansion. "My mother was sleeping in the house one night in 1990 when she said she was awakened by a really cold presence," Liz says. "My mother is not one to exaggerate. A lot of unexplained things have happened here."

The wife of a previous owner also reported "strange things" occurring. She says maids felt very uncomfortable in certain areas of the house, especially in the hyphens connecting wings. There also has been a persistent legend of a strong scent of lavender in one of the upper floor rooms, although no source for the odor has ever been found. A long-time housekeeper told of being in the dining room one day when a double swinging door opened and closed by itself. There was no one else there.

Bobby Swineford, who has worked at the plantation, off and on, for more than 40 years, says that in the 1970s, when his two sons were in the third grade, one had a chilling experience in a brick dependency adjacent to the main building. "He was awakened at about two in the morning by the sounds of someone walking — someone in heavy boots, dragging one foot," Bobby says. "He was petrified. He got out of bed and ran toward the front door. As he did, he went through a frigid cold spot. He said whatever it was making the sounds followed him outside. He then ran back in and hid under his covers. My other son said he had similar encounters. He told me it sounded like the footsteps were impregnated in the floor. They made thumping sounds."

Bobby himself became unnerved one night when he was in the basement area getting some steaks out of a freezer. "There was a door there with a glass top. I began hearing some soft tapping sounds. Something was tapping on the glass part of the door. It sounded like the eraser end of a lead pencil. I thought at first someone was playing a trick on me, but I checked around. There was no one else there."

Others have said they have heard the sounds of furniture being moved around upstairs in the house when no one was upstairs. Once, a housekeeper was washing some linens in the washing machine. She left them there. When she came back later, the linens were mysteriously hanging from overhead pipes. If it was a ghost who did this, it appeared to be a tidy one.

One day a workman asked to use a downstairs bathroom. He came racing out of the house seconds later, his eyes bulging. He said he heard footsteps and furniture being moved, although no one else was in the house. He stammered that there was "something evil" in there and declared the next time he had to go, he'd go in the bushes.

There are three interesting portraits in the house. One is of Maria Byrd, half sister of Evelyn Byrd. It formerly was at Westover in the days of the "Black Swan," William Byrd, II. Another portrait is of Martha Blount, said to have been the friend and sweetheart of Alexander Pope. She is seated at a harpsichord and holds a scroll of music on her lap.

The third painting, which hangs over the fireplace in the library, is of two young boys. They are of two of the sons of William Byrd Harrison — Benjamin and Randolph. Benjamin was killed in the Civil War and Randolph lost a leg in the war.

In the winter of 1989, Liz Dehan was visiting Upper Brandon when it was still a private residence. She traditionally took photos of her two daughters, Hillary and Caroline, then 7 and 3, for annual Christmas cards. She had the girls sit in front of the fireplace in the library, beneath the portrait of Benjamin and Randolph Harrison. A fire was going.

When the photos were developed they showed a most curious thing. Liz had taken a series of several shots. The first one of the girls was fine. But as the series progressed, a cloud-like swirl seemed to evolve out of the fireplace and surround her daughters, the final one virtually enveloped them. Liz says there was no smoke or mist in the house. She has no explanation for the phenomenon.

Nor does anyone else associated with Upper Brandon know what spirit or spirits might make their presence known. One could speculate that the ghost of Randolph Harrison could be the source of the heavy boot tread with the dragging foot. It is believed that he died in the house. Or could it be Benjamin Harrison returning to his home after dying such a tragic death across the James River at Malvern Hill? Or is it a former housekeeper or slave who comes back to tidy things up? Or all of them?

Whatever or whichever, Upper Brandon is a handsome old home on a beautiful site overlooking the James. It is open for a couple of days each spring during Virginia's annual garden week — and well worth a visit.

CHAPTER 37

A Tragic Toast at Brandon

In a book on the homes and gardens of Virginia, it is written about Brandon Plantation that, "it does not seem possible that so much loveliness can belong to one old house." Boxwood hedges, more than a century old, flank this superb manor home on a 4,500-acre farm located in Prince George County on the south side of the James River between Surry and Hopewell. Here, today, a dazzling array of flowers, every hue of the rainbow, gracefully coexist with giant elms, ancient yews, hollies, tulip poplars, dogwoods, redbuds, and varieties of magnolias, pecans, oaks, horse chestnuts, hickories, persimmons, hawthorns and locusts — to form magnificent gardens, open to the public, and leading to the banks of the James River.

The estate itself actually dates to 1616 when a vast grant of land was made to Captain John Martin who accompanied John Smith on the first voyage to Virginia. In 1720, the land was acquired by Nathaniel Harrison. The main part of the house was built about 1765 by Nathaniel Harrison II as a wedding present for his son, Benjamin, who was a friend of Thomas Jefferson. It is believed that Jefferson designed this center structure. The two extensive wings of Brandon postdate Harrison ownership and were added to the main portion, creating a sweeping house frontage of 210 feet. The walls were riddled with gunfire during the Civil War, and, for a time, Brandon was occupied by Union troops. However, except for some living room paneling which was ripped out and used for firewood, little substantive damage was done.

During the latter part of the 18th century, and for most of the

19th, Brandon was a prime site for the gala social life enjoyed by plantation owners of the times. Lavish parties, dances and weddings were held here and the rich and well known gentlemen and ladies arrived in ornate coaches, and by boat from the north side of the river, from such great mansions as Shirley, Berkeley and Westover. It was from such an aura of refined gaiety that the main character in what evolved into a haunting tragedy emerges.

Her name was Jane Evelyn Harrison, the 18-year-old daughter of William Byrd Harrison of Williamsburg. She has been described as a charming heiress endowed with position and beauty, who, according to writer Hubert Davis who documented that era, "used her capricious blue eyes, winning smile, and every feminine wile she could summon to entrap and smash the hearts of young men." She was, in a very special sense, a real-life Scarlett O'Hara.

It was at a typically jubilant spring dance at Brandon that Jane met and immediately entranced a young Frenchman named Pierre Bondurant. He fell hopelessly in love with the fickle belle, and while details of their short but intense courtship are sketchy, he repeatedly proposed marriage to her. By applying an intriguing feminine mystique beyond her years, she left Pierre more or less dangling. She told him, as he was leaving for a lengthy trip to Paris, that such a union would only be possible with the expressed approval of her father, knowing very well that this would be all but impossible. Pierre was persistent, suggesting that they elope to France, but Jane demurred, saying that she planned to spend the summer at Brandon, partying with her friends.

Saddened, but ever hopeful, Pierre departed for Paris. He had hardly been there a month when he received a letter from a friend, the news of which devastatingly tore at his very fiber. William Byrd Harrison had announced the engagement of Jane. She was to wed Ralph Fitzhugh Cocke of Bacon's Castle in late November! The wedding was to be one of the grandest events of the year. It was to be held at Brandon so as to accommodate more than 100 guests, including Pierre Bondurant. And so, on the last day of November, a sumptuous feast was held, featuring the finest foods and the best wines and liquors in the commonwealth.

Curiously, Pierre asked the prospective groom if he could propose the first toast at the wedding dinner and his request was granted. "Whatever fate may be," he said, "and this day alone will tell, may both of you be happy and free from sorrow, malice and ill." No one could imagine at the time what fate Pierre had in mind. The wedding took place at 4 p.m., and was followed by an extravagant reception.

At some point during the festivities, Pierre pulled Jane aside, handed her a glass of champagne, and asked her to exchange toasts with him. Delighted that he seemed to show no lingering bitterness from their past "fling," she agreed, and they each drank to the other's happiness. Just then Ralph walked up, unnoticed by the couple, and overheard Pierre offer a strange poem to Jane: 'Twas you I loved when we first met, I loved you then and I love you yet; 'Tis vain for me to try to forget, Lo! Both of us could die before sunset."

Obviously embarrassed when he realized Ralph had heard him, Pierre gulped down his champagne, made excuses, and nervously left the house. By the time all but the house guests had gone, Jane had become deathly ill and collapsed on the drawing room floor, gasping for breath. She was whisked to an upstairs bedroom and died that evening. Although it wasn't known then, she had been poisoned! As author Davis noted, "a veil of silence and sadness descended on everyone."

Oddly, as Jane's body was being prepared for burial it was

Brandon

noticed that her wedding ring was missing. No one could shed any light on this little mystery and she was laid to rest. A few days later, a messenger arrived from Williamsburg with the shocking news that Pierre Bondurant had been found dead in his carriage when it arrived in Williamsburg on the night of the wedding. Even more discomforting was the fact that Jane's wedding ring had been found — in Pierre's pocket!

The mistress of Brandon, Elizabeth Richardson Harrison, Jane's aunt, in an extraordinarily peculiar gesture, declared that the ring now bore a curse, and she had it embedded in the plaster on the ceiling above the spot where Jane had fallen.

Over the years following, there were periodic reports from residents, guests and servants, of seeing a wispy apparition of a young woman, in a flowing white gown, who seemed to appear only in late November, and Brandon slowly began gaining a reputation as being haunted. In fact, when Helen Lynne Thomas became mistress of the plantation, fully two generations after the tragedy, the real estate agent had casually referred to a "resident ghost."

That fall, Helen met the spectral being first-hand. It was on a stormy dark night as she was walking past the family cemetery. Amidst the weathered old tombstones she got a glimpse of a wraith-like figure seemingly drifting toward the main house. She trembled with fear, nearly fainted, then regained her composure and hurried into the great hall. There, she heard a thud which sounded like something heavy had fallen in the adjacent drawing room. She walked across the hall, opened the door, and saw that some plaster had fallen from the ceiling.

And then, as her eyes adjusted to the blackness, she saw something else — the same ethereal, white-robed phantom she had imagined she had seen outside. It appeared to hover about the room for a few seconds and then kind of settled over the pile of plaster as if it were searching for something. Helen could hardly breathe. Then either the door or a loose floorboard creaked and the figure straightened up, slid toward the door, and disappeared.

As it did, Helen screamed, and then fainted dead away. When she was aroused, more than an hour later, she told members of her family and the servants who had rushed to her what had happened. It was then that one of the servants, Hattie McCoy, told her about Jane Harrison and Pierre Bondurant. Hattie's grandmother had been at Brandon on the fateful wedding day.

After she recovered, Helen sorted through the fallen plaster